ALWYN JAMES spent hi n the Welsh valley town of T anges of scenery, firstly three ye the flat landscape of East Anglia and then ten years as editor of an industrial magazine in London, he arrived in 1970, almost by accident, in Scotland. In the years since then, his career has been all about communication, as editor, writer, press officer and internal publications chief, the last two with The Royal Bank of Scotland.

An unapologetic dilettante, he has, in addition to his books, written articles in the Scottish press on subjects as diverse as Enrico Caruso and Scottish banknotes, the explorer Alexander Mackenzie and Welsh rugby. Within the Royal Bank he is better known in a Jekyll and Hyde combination – jovial TV presenter and sadistic setter of quizzes.

His flurry of writing since semi-retirement from the Bank has produced a film script of Caruso's last days, a TV adaptation of a Victorian tear-jerker, a romantic crime novel – and boxes of rejection slips.

He and his wife Jean, the inspiration behind *Scottish Roots*, have now established something of a dynasty in Edinburgh, with daughters-in-law and grandchildren swelling the numbers carrying on the Tredegar James name to nine, although two sons have fled the nest to Bavaria and Sweden.

SCOTTISH ROOTS

THE STEP-BY-STEP GUIDE
TO TRACING YOUR SCOTTISH ANCESTORS

ALWYN JAMES

Luath Press Limited

EDINBURGH

www.luath.co.uk

To Jean and Popsy,
their smiles were Irish but their roots were Scottish.

To Helen, Chris and Sara,
the latest twigs on the tree.

First Published by Macdonald Publishers 1981
Revised Edition Published by The Saltire Society 1995
New Revised Edition 2002
Reprinted 2003
Reprinted 2005

The paper used in this book is acid-free, neutral-sized and recyclable.
It is made from low chlorine pulps produced in a low energy,
low emission manner from sustainable forests.

Printed and bound by
Bookmarque Ltd., Croydon

Typeset in 11.5 point Meta by
S. Fairgrieve, Edinburgh, 0131 658 1763

Contents

Appendices

INTRODUCTION TO THE NEW *SCOTTISH ROOTS* – because so much has changed

When *Scottish Roots* first appeared in 1981, its success surprised most genealogy-watchers, not least the author and publishers. It had clearly found not just a gap but a vacuum in the market. It has in the intervening years had more than a dozen reprints and been published separately in Canada and in the USA, for the latter market by a publisher appropriately located in Gretna. Louisiana not Scotland.

I became the rather bemused target for a fascinating flood of letters from ancestor-hunters all over the world and at home was dragooned into taking on the unsought role of pundit. I willingly accepted invitations to address the growing number of societies and clubs with a keen interest in Scottish heritage and, if I lacked the expertise of many professionals, I came to believe that I had enthusiasm and encouragement, if little else, to transmit.

Such was the total involvement of these Scottish gatherings that I can honestly say that I never came away from one of my own lectures without having learnt more than the audience.

The worldwide nature of the reaction is best illustrated by Bob Leitch, one of the guinea pigs in my two case histories. Bob received letters from long-lost relatives as far afield as Australia and North America who somehow picked up the references in *Scottish Roots*.

The popularity of family history, combined with the almost supernatural powers of computers, both business and personal, has meant faster and more significant changes in the past decade than in previous periods and this has had the effect of demanding a complete rethink of *Scottish Roots*.

The new book sets out to balance the traditional messages and principles of the 1981 book with the revolution that has taken place in the record offices and libraries and in the homes of ancestor-hunters.

The same magic which allows the person in the travel agency to tell you immediately that there are two seats left on a plane for Naples and, when you get there, lets you take money out of your Glasgow bank account from a hole in the wall in Sorrento, can perform even more amazing tricks for the ancestor-hunter – and do so in your own home.

No less significantly, the places where you are likely to be looking for information – the libraries, record offices and most notably New Register House – have also been able to unleash the potential of twenty-first-century information technology to streamline and expand their own procedures and practices. This means that, while the store of information remains much the same, the number of places where you can tap into it has exploded.

The great treasuries of the General Register Office (GRO) and the National Archives of Scotland (NAS) remain unchallenged, but there are many more places where you can access large chunks of their goodies, from your own PC at home to the reference and local libraries which, in response to the popularity of genealogy, now carry computer, microfiche and microfilm material. While not elbowing out GRO and NAS, this has made it possible to prepare much more material in advance of a visit to Edinburgh.

It is not only the local libraries that have set out to cater for the interest in family history. Very many more collections of material relating to localities or trades are being assembled and displayed to the public. These can take the form of precisely targeted exhibitions, permanent or temporary, or even of new, fully fledged museums. At all levels, these provide a valuable resource for the ancestor-hunter.

Again, reflecting the popularity of heritage studies, Scotland has now got very much better coverage as far as family history societies are concerned. When *Scottish Roots* first appeared the coverage was sparse compared with England, growth perhaps held back by the dominant clan societies. Now, however, there is barely a corner of Scotland without its own family history society, all of them productive, but some more prolific than others.

These give the ancestor-hunter more and more opportunities to share enthusiasms, successes and setbacks and make the hobby a sociable rather than a solitary one.

There is indeed a bright future for the past.

Alwyn James
Edinburgh

INTRODUCTION TO THE 1981 EDITION
– because so much remains the same

When a Welshman married to an Irish girl lands up writing a book on how to trace your Scottish ancestors, he owes his readers something of an explanation.

I came to Edinburgh in April 1970, along with my Dublin-born wife, four sons born in London, a degree from an English university and a Welsh birth certificate. These, it appeared, qualified me to edit the business and political magazine *Scotland*. This I dutifully did for the next three-and-a-half years. And that was time enough to get me (and the rest of the family) firmly hooked on Scotland, its history and people, its politics and potential, its culture and even its rugby. I might add that I had already appreciated one of its great exports, whisky, and never got to grips with another, golf.

When my wife, Jean, with green eyes and Irish lilt, announced that her grandfather was Scottish, we sniffed some real tartan roots and Jean set off in what little spare time she had (in between looking after me and the ravenous boys) to see what could be found in the Scottish records.

I started work as a freelance, Jean went out to work and I had in those early months a lot of what is euphemistically called 'thinking time' on my hands.

I decided to take up where Jean had left off. Encouraged by the benefit of an unusual Scottish name – you don't find a Balbirnie on every street corner – I plunged into the depths of New Register House and within hours had contracted that appalling and increasingly common disease of ancestor-hunting, a disease for which there is no known cure.

Ancestor-hunting, even in this form, one step removed

from my own family, had everything: the magnetism of the puzzle, the thrill of the chase, the challenge of the unknown and the very real sense of exploring territory which has not been surveyed and measured, logged and plotted by all and sundry. Add to this the fact that it is your own ancestors you are identifying and learning about and you will get an inkling of the power of the addiction.

Now, of course, is the age of the ancestor-hunter. For decades, people had ceased to bother about their forebears – especially in the teeming urban centres – and I think I was perhaps typical of my generation in not being able to go back beyond my grandparents. Searching for forebears had been the preserve of those whose families had done great or dastardly deeds, had signed treaties or led armies. Today, there is an intrinsic interest in roots, no matter how lowly or unsung the people involved.

There is still a thrill to be got from finding someone out of the ordinary in your family tree. I have not yet managed to unearth such a one, although I get some pleasure from seeing snooker star Ray Reardon dangling from one of the lower branches. But there is now no longer the quest for a rightful title or desire to link on to the aristocracy in genealogical endeavour; it is a matter of roots for roots' sake.

If now is the time to be looking for ancestors, then Scotland is the place. Having done a little family research on my Welsh roots, I had had some experience of the system south of Hadrian's Wall – slow, frustrating and expensive.

Seeing just what was available in Scotland opened my eyes to the tremendous advantages Scots and the descendants of Scots have over their neighbours in the British Isles. The country has a rich and colourful past by any standards and few countries, if any, can match Scotland's past two hundred and fifty years, precisely the period most of you are going to be concerned with in your ancestor-hunting.

What is truly staggering is the extent to which this tapestry of politics and industry, art and culture, invention and community is an open book to those who want to find out just what their ancestors were doing when Scotland was passing through those two and a half momentous centuries.

Scottish Roots is an attempt to show what can be achieved by Scots who have not yet become aware of the rich legacy of records and documents which can allow even people from the humblest origins to span those centuries.

It is not intended to provide the exhaustive and definitive guide to all the many sources. A number of extremely good books already perform that function. It will, I hope, give enough of the bald and basic facts – what information exists, where it is kept, how you can get hold of it, what you will find when you see it, how to log the information – to make you feel at home in the environment of papers and documents, indexes and official records, to encourage you to make a serious, but not necessarily solemn, search for the people who have gone into the manufacture of that unique product – you.

Alwyn James
Edinburgh
1981

ONE

Genealogy Begins at Home

The work you can get down to at home straightaway can simplify your ancestor-hunting later on.

> 'Tom was always singing and when he was older he used to go for voice training and started singing operatic pieces. There used to be a chip cart coming around in the evenings. The man driving and serving was Italian. We all looked forward to a half-penny bag of chips which was delicious, but Tom was more concerned with trying out his Italian arias and following the cart all around town.'

Genealogy, like charity, begins at home. The information above, referring to the pursuits of an uncle of mine just after the 1914-18 War, came as the result of the work I did on building up a family history not in some large repository of documents but at home. And you too can get down to the business of ancestor-hunting immediately, without waiting for your next trip to Edinburgh or even your next visit to Scotland.

The work you can do at home is, moreover, just as important as any of the poring over records or reference books in the libraries or record offices where you will be spending much of your time later in the quest. Indeed, these first few steps can help clarify in your mind just what it is you are tackling and set patterns for your later work. This will prove invaluable when the volume of information gets greater and might threaten to intimidate you. It can certainly help you make the most of your time when you come face-to-face with large numbers of documents.

FIRST STEP

Take a sheet of paper, not too mean in size. You can get started right away on that intriguing jigsaw of a hobby where you start with one little piece (yourself) and from that centre-point work upwards in ever widening vistas, ahead and to the side. Each step will give you more and more pieces to look for, occasionally resulting in a dead end, but never reaching the borders of the infinite picture you are constructing.

Write down your own name and work upwards in a simple little line chart of parents, grandparents and even have a bash at your great-grandparents. You should end up with something like the diagram shown alongside.

Now try filling in a few dates of births and marriages and deaths. And when you've done that, how about some addresses and occupations?

When you've got into the swing of things, start branching out into aunts and uncles, brothers and sisters and see just how far you can get. You will probably land up with a very congested network.

You may be an exception to the general rule but I'll assume for the moment that you are not and that four basic comments can apply to your chart:

1 You have lots of names in your own generation, not so many in your parents' generation 'band' and few in your grandparents' band.
2 You won't go back very far beyond your grandparents.
3 Your dates and addresses will be very vague.
4 You will have surprised yourself at the gaps as far as such things as, say, your grandmothers' maiden names are concerned.

For all those limitations, the chart will clearly set targets for your work of ancestor-hunting: to fill those gaps, clarify those

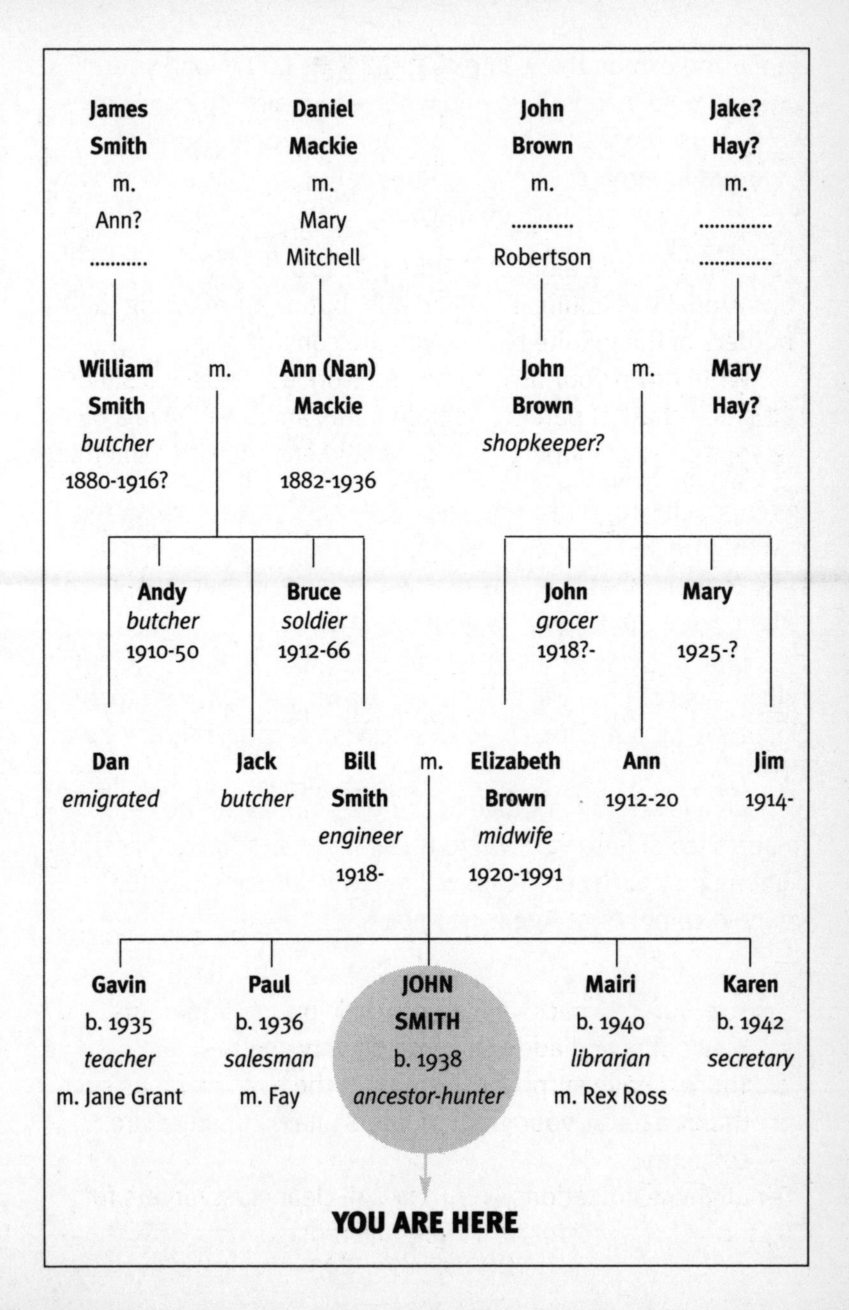
James
Smith
m.
Ann?
....
Daniel
Mackie
m.
Mary
Mitchell
John
Brown
m.
....
Robertson
Jake?
Hay?
m.
....
....
William
Smith
butcher
1880-1916?
m.
Ann (Nan)
Mackie
1882-1936
John
Brown
shopkeeper?
m.
Mary
Hay?
Andy
butcher
1910-50
Bruce
soldier
1912-66
John
grocer
1918?-
Mary
1925-?
Dan
emigrated
Jack
butcher
Bill
Smith
engineer
1918-
m.
Elizabeth
Brown
midwife
1920-1991
Ann
1912-20
Jim
1914-
Gavin
b. 1935
teacher
m. Jane Grant
Paul
b. 1936
salesman
m. Fay
JOHN
SMITH
b. 1938
ancestor-hunter
Mairi
b. 1940
librarian
m. Rex Ross
Karen
b. 1942
secretary
YOU ARE HERE

dates, and extend the whole chart back as far beyond your grandparents as possible. And when you realise the pace at which those ancestors multiply – four grandparents, eight great-grandparents, sixteen great-great-grandparents and so on – you will see that, even discounting the brothers and sisters of all those people, there are a lot of ancestors up there waiting to be discovered. You should, with an average amount of luck and a variable amount of effort, have little difficulty in getting back to 1800 – and at that date there may very well have been 64 or 128 people on whom you can blame your genes!

But patience, we're not there yet. Let's get back to basics.

Having exhausted your own fund of knowledge, it is time to get in touch with those relatives who can add to your list, tell you that Uncle Jack was a railwayman, that his sister went to New Zealand, that Ned was married twice. And, perhaps, even extend your chart into new generation bands

Some of those relatives will be living near at hand: go and talk to them. Some will be a bus-ride away: go and visit them. Some will be out of reach as far as a visit is concerned: write to them.

There is no way in which I can over-emphasise the importance of getting down to these tasks as soon as possible. Aunt Aggie's birth certificate will be available for study for years to come; Aunt Aggie may not.

WHAT TO LOOK FOR

You will find out from the start that diplomacy and tact are useful attributes to the genealogist, but that shyness or reticence are distinct handicaps. At this stage, some books dwell on the problems of getting information from elderly relatives. These difficulties are, to a large extent, imaginary, most older folk relishing the chance to talk about Auld Lang Syne, long-dead relatives and distant kinsmen!

In essence, you are at this stage looking for three distinct types of information:

1. NAMES AND PLACES

You will be keen to add to the information that you were trying to piece together in your first tentative chart – who married whom, what they did, how many children they had, what they worked at. Older relatives will, by the very nature of things, be strong in those bands where you have been weak.

2. DOCUMENTS AND PHOTOGRAPHS

Over the years, your family, just like any other, must have acquired letters, diaries, photographs, bank books, life assurance policies, deeds and what have you. The relatives you are going to contact may be able to help you locate these. They may know where the family Bible went, who got the only photograph of great-uncle George in his army uniform, where Billy's letters from Ypres landed up. The female members of the family are more likely hoarders than the men.

3. REMINISCENCES

Arguably, the most important of these three is the story of the family as seen by any older relative. And that person doesn't have to be a 90-year-old to make his or her story worth listening to. I make no apology for repeating that in this case, as to a lesser extent in the first two types, there is an immediacy in the matter. The sooner you start getting in touch, the better.

FACE TO FACE

There are many roles that ancestor-seekers are called upon to play in their hobby. In the business of 'pumping' relatives, it is necessary to acquire at some speed the skills of the journalist. The task is eased in most cases by the willingness, if not eagerness, of most elderly relatives to respond to any sign of interest from the younger generation! Again, you will, from the tips above and from your own 'tree' sketch, have a clear idea of just what it is you are looking for.

The taking of notes does, however, pose a problem to anyone not used to this deceptively difficult task. If at all possible, get hold of a tape-recorder rather than plump for note-taking. Unless you are fast and experienced, this is a bit of a gamble, as most of us find difficulty in keeping up with even moderate conversation. There is nothing more off-putting to the elderly aunt in full flow than to have you saying 'Slow down', 'What did you say?' or 'Could you stop a moment while I get that down?' Remember: you are aiming to record a conversation, not a concert, and quality of sound is less important than a simple, unobtrusive machine that will not put off the person whose reminiscences you are taping. For the same reason, go for the long-playing tapes that will cut down the need to interrupt a flow of words to change a tape.

If you have to take notes, minimise the problems by accepting that it is only the key points you want to record. In this case, as soon as you get home, go over the notes, expanding and clarifying any points while your recollection of the conversation is still fresh.

So off we go. Whether you are using tape-recorder or notes, or indeed a combination of both, it is best to get the conversation under way without either. Your own efforts at compiling a family tree will provide a good starting-off point and, as most people love to be able to add to or correct someone else's work, this should get your aged relative going.

The information which starts to flow will provide a good and natural link with your request to produce notebook and/or tape recorder, and with a bit of luck Aunt Ethel or Uncle Jimmy will be in full swing and in no mood to be intimidated by either. Incidentally, with mention of Aunt and Uncle, it is worth underlining here the benefits of getting two relatives together for the interview. You'll be surprised at the way in which the two will spark off lines of thought one with another. The disadvantages – mainly difficulty in keeping control of the conversation – are more than outweighed by the very real advantages that emerge.

NAMES AND PLACES

Start your recorder or head the page of your notebook with the date, place and the people involved in the conversation. Concentrate on the top end of your own chart and, when someone's name crops up, get the information flowing with such queries as 'Where did he live?', 'What did he do?', 'Whom did he marry?' or 'Did they have any children?'

There are a few points to try and remember during this section of the interview:

1. Try and establish dates. If there is difficulty in getting these with any degree of accuracy, try at least to relate events in your family not only to obvious 'landmarks', such as the Wars or the Coronation, but also to each other, such as 'Did that happen after they moved to Carlisle?' or 'Was Donald born at that point?'
2. In particular, try and get some semblance of order in the people mentioned. Your elderly relative will happily reel off aunts and uncles and cousins, but to make sense out of this at a later stage it would help to know the answers to such questions as 'Who was the youngest sister?' or 'Was she older than you?'
3. When it comes to a question of the jobs of some of the people, try and find out who they worked for, rather than just the fact that Uncle Jimmy was a carpenter. Was he a master-carpenter? Did he run his own business? Did he work for someone else? If someone was in the army, which regiment? If someone was a teacher, at which school? A railway worker, on which line?
4. One aspect of occupation which is often neglected in such records as marriage entries is the question of what the young women did. Once married, the role of a housewife took up most of a woman's time and working wives were not as common as today, but before marriage the woman might be working in a shop or a mill – and your elderly relative might remember.

You may well be one of the increasing number of camcorder owners. In future, I am sure that video footage will become a central resource for family history. At this stage however, people and especially the older generations are distracted by camcorders to an extent which can seriously inhibit communication. I would therefore strongly recommend that, while you should get footage of older members of the family reminiscing, film this after the real interview. This is often how professional programme makers do it.

DOCUMENTS AND PHOTOGRAPHS

I mentioned earlier that your family must have acquired over the years a host of bits of paper that you would like to get your hands on. Equally certainly, a huge proportion of these will have been jettisoned, lost or destroyed. But there will undoubtedly be some around somewhere – and your aged relative might be able to help locate them. It is not enough to ask bluntly, 'Where are the family papers?' Try going through a list of the sort of things you are looking for – and don't be self-conscious about producing an actual check-list to read out. It shows you are in earnest – and might also jog the memory when specific items are mentioned. Here is the sort of checklist you may like to start with:

1 Diaries, letters, notebooks – the real cream – and don't be too disappointed if you don't find any!
2 Copies of Birth, Marriage and Death Certificates – the more you can collect now, the fewer you have to hunt for in the official files.
3 Wills, deeds, insurance policies.
4 Photographs – again real gems. In particular, look for family groupings. A wedding photograph, for example, is ideal, especially if you can find relatives to name the people shown. You will almost certainly sigh in frustration at the number of times you find photographs with no indication as to who is shown in them. Don't fume: just go and caption your own family album.

5 Books owned by earlier relatives – and it is not just the family Bible that is likely to contain information on the fly-leaf; many old books will contain addresses, perhaps a forgotten maiden name. My sister-in-law has a prayer-book which belonged to her grandmother. It contained: evidence of a previous marriage, the surname on the fly-leaf being neither the maiden name nor the only married name we knew for the lady, an address and a date, and five cuttings from newspapers relating to deaths of friends and relatives.
6 Books or articles or poems written by relatives even if not related to family matters.
7 Details of any land owned or court cases involving relatives – which will lead you to records and documents held by specific offices.
8 Any information regarding schools or universities attended, army or navy service – again helping you move on to outside sources of documentation.
9 Any other work similar to one you are attempting to produce. Don't be put off if you are told that Old Jake did all this before. Even if you manage to get hold of his records, you can bet that he had still left plenty for you to do!

But, as always in this business, stop and ponder. Are there any unusual things you should be looking for? The list above is general and cannot cope with the little oddities that come to light in every family. I am still searching for an old 78rpm recording made by that uncle I mentioned in the first sentence of this chapter. Anyone out there with a shellac record of 'An Italian Salad' by the St David Singers?

I have already mentioned the camcorder and it is worth

remembering that it is very effective to store still images – photographs, documents, maps, charts and so on – on the video tapes to be used in conjunction with moving images.

REMINISCENCES

Talk to anyone who has got hooked on this ancestor-hunting and you'll find that he or she will have a wistful regret at not having spoken to – or perhaps listened to – now long-dead relatives who had so much to tell about the family roots. Get down to the real task of doing what you can with the relatives who are available, especially in this matter of memories. 'Old men forget,' said the English Bard, but it is equally true that they remember – that is what you are interested in.

Once again, it is important in your role of catalyst to be specific. Don't just ask 'What do you remember of your childhood?' Try precise triggers such as 'Where did you go to school?', 'How did you get there?', 'What do you remember about your teachers?', 'Your friends?' Find out about the home and the family: 'How many rooms did you have?', 'Who slept where?', 'What do you remember most about your brothers and sisters as children?', 'Where did you go on your holidays?' This is often a surprisingly fruitful source of information, as in the days before Benidorm and Butlin's children usually travelled to relatives for their holidays. It may even open up some branches which had not emerged earlier in the conversation.

In the long run, the style of the interview will depend to a large extent more on the character of you and your relative rather than on these notes – but they will help you discipline your approach.

TACKLING DISTANT RELATIVES

The problem of the distant relative – and that refers to geography rather than relationship or temperament! – is a formidable one. It is impossible to get the rapport and feedback of a face-to-face chat, but it is possible to extract a great deal of information by post. Again you are dealing with those three basic areas of investigation and again you should try and tackle all of them precisely and effectively.

Don't forget to send along:

1. Your own efforts at compiling a chart. Ask if your relative can add any names, dates, places, occupations.
2. Your check-list of documents and photographs. If you locate a source of family photographs, your relative may very well be reluctant to commit them to you and the postman – so think about footing the bill for the neighbourhood photographer or copyshop to copy them.
3. Blank sheets of paper with a simple, single reminiscence question at the top: 'What do you remember about your school?', 'Your Church?', 'Your house?', 'Your brothers?', 'Your sisters?', 'Your aunts?', 'Your uncles?' Even be specific enough to name individuals. One such sheet I sent to an eighty-four-year-old aunt produced the quote given at the beginning of this chapter and that is a piece of information which would never have emerged from the records of births, marriages and deaths.
4. A stamped addressed envelope. It is surprising just how effective it can be to make a reply as simple as possible, especially to older people who may require a long walk to get an envelope or stamp. Those blank sheets with headings also help out here.

You are now well on the way to an attack on the massive stores of documents and records, but there is still much that can be done at home to prepare for and simplify that project.

PREPARING TO RECEIVE INFORMATION

For many people, the study of documents and the making of notes is a new and daunting prospect. One aim of this book is to help you cope with the mass of facts and dates which will soon be coming your way by showing you exactly what you can expect, what you should look for and how you should handle the information you collect.

There is no one answer to how you should log the results of your research, but here are two suggestions.

I strongly recommend the **family group sheet** in which, as the name suggests, the unit is the family, with husband and wife (with names of their parents) fully detailed along with all children. This gives a very clear picture of all groupings and in particular will show at a glance the name patterns which, as I outline in Appendix III, were a helpful and widespread feature of Scottish families during the period we shall be studying.

There is for simplicity sake an attraction in the use of **individual sheets** in which a sheet is devoted to a single person rather than to a family group. An example of the sheet is shown overleaf. The amount of space given allows you to include full details of jobs, addresses and ancillary but often helpful details such as witnesses, who was the informant, i.e. who provided the information to the registrar, causes of death and references to the Census returns, and it still leaves room for the inevitable marginal notes, referring for example to wills, directory entries or legal cases. The generation band is clearly marked on each sheet, counting yourself as 1, your parents as 2, your grandparents as 3 and

FAMILY GROUP SHEET

HUSBAND		WIFE
BIRTH		
Date	....	....
Place	....	....
BAPTISM		
Date	....	....
Place	....	....
Report/witnesses	....	....
MARRIAGE/BANNS		
Date	....	....
Place	....	....
Address	....	....
Age and condition	....	....
Witnesses	....	....
DEATH/BURIAL		
Date	....	....
Place	....	....
Cause of death	....	....
Address	....	....
Age and occupation	....	....
Buried at	....	....
Reported by	....	....
PARENTS		
Father	....	....
Mother	....	....

CHILDREN

1	....	5	....
2	....	6	....
3	....	7	....
4	....	8	....

INDIVIDUAL FACT SHEET

Name ....

BIRTH/BAPTISM

Date .... Place ....

Father .... Mother ....

Report by/witnesses ....

MARRIAGE/BANNS

Date .... Place ....

Address ....

Age and condition ....

Father .... Mother ....

Spouse

Father .... Mother ....

Witnesses ....

DEATH/BURIAL

Date .... Place ....

Cause of death ....

Address ....

Age and occupation ....

Buried at ....

Spouse

Parents ....

Reported by ....

CHILDREN with year of birth/death

1 .... 5 ....

2 .... 6 ....

3 .... 7 ....

4 .... 8 ....

CENSUS address

1841 .... 1871 ....

1851 .... 1881 ....

1861 .... 1891 ....

GENERATION BAND ....

so on and sheets can, at any stage, be arranged together into family groupings as required.

No matter which of these approaches you go for, the sheets can be provided in quantity by typing or neatly drawing out the form onto an A4 sheet of paper – 297 by 210mm, the standard business letter size. If you have a PC, print off batches as you need them. If not, get them duplicated at one of the many copy-service centres which are available in most towns. If there is any problem here, a local business firm might very well do the job for you at a reasonable charge. Fifty family sheets would keep you busy for a while, the individual sheets clearly needing more, perhaps as many as 200.

These sheets will form the basis of your master records and should be kept at home to receive the information you collect from personal and official records.

There has, however, in recent years been a dramatic new addition to the array of equipment in the average home which can revolutionise the keeping of your records. The TV has been joined by the video-recorder, the telephone by the answer-machine, the oven by the microwave, the washing machine by the dishwasher. But none of these can match the impact of the personal computer, the PC. Invariably infiltrated into the home by the younger element, the avid game-players, the keen student or the thrusting young businessperson, the PC offers an astonishing range of capabilities which are most mouth-watering to the family historian.

This has not escaped the attention of the producers of software and a number of very effective packages are available targeted directly at the genealogist/family historian. The best advice is to look at the advertisements in some of the popular PC-user magazines and send off for details.

The magic that allowed the book-keeper the miracle of being able to type in each month's figures and see them find their way into the right places in his accounts and produce totals and subtotals automatically is now available to the builder of pedigrees and family trees.

It will often involve having to learn new skills, but all the effort is well worth it. Very few families are without enthusiastic computer-literate youngsters eager to pass on the benefits of their experience to their elders.

We'll see some of the more amazing tricks of the PC later but at this stage let's concentrate on that family history package as it is an aid that you can tap into immediately. And it will certainly save you a lot of headaches as far as marshalling a growing amount of data is concerned.

TWO

The PC Genealogy Package

A magical filing system at your fingertips can make child's play out of mountains of information.

The ancestor-hunter with a PC has an enormous start over the person who is setting out on the quest without one. As you will see later, there are many aids that the PC can bring to the search for ancestors, from access to the most amazing computer databases to the more mundane magic of producing attractive typescripts and charts.

While most of these kick in when you have done a fair amount of the fundamental research work, one aid can be recruited immediately: a PC genealogy software package. A large number of products are available either by mail order through the computer magazines or from a store like PC World.

WHAT DOES THE SOFTWARE GIVE YOU?

In essence, it can eat up even the most voluminous quantities of genealogical information, relate it to existing information, file everything in easily understood relationships and make it all easily accessible at the touch of a couple of keys.

HOW DOES IT DO THAT?

It is invariably based on the well tried and tested family unit method and the best way to understand that is simply to set the ball rolling.

The software will normally give you a sample family setup to let you get the general idea. This can be fictitious or, in the case of the package I use, a real family. The US origins of the package show in the fact that the family chosen is the Kennedys.

You then get your starter screen – the equivalent of the blank piece of paper I mentioned at the very beginning of this book.

What will strike you immediately, however, is that it is far more helpful than that frightening empty sheet. Stripped of the usual PC 'furniture', it shows the basic unit for the entire system, something along these lines:

1. Twin boxes for a theoretical husband and wife pairing, husband/male partner to the left, wife/female partner to the right.
2. In each box, a series of essential details including place and date of birth, place and date of christening, place and date of death, place and date of burial, history, sources.
3. Above each partner a box indicating marriage place/date and, higher up, a pair of boxes showing the parents.
4. Below each pair of partners a 'fence' containing their children. A useful convention is that males have a squared box and females a rounded one.

This screen is the simple building block on which the entire system is built up. By the time you are finished, that single screen will be one of perhaps a hundred or so. Just imagine the problems that would pose if we were talking handwritten sheets.

Even for the most computer illiterate of us, the system is simple and easily absorbed.

To get the hang of things, start by putting your own details into the blank screen. Click on the 'Enter' button and you will be offered a drop-down choice.

If you're a male, go for 'Husband's Facts', a female for 'Wife's Facts'. You'll be offered a pro forma into which you key in all those essential details I mentioned above. Fill in the Facts you know, leave blank the ones you don't – you can always add them later on.

Save the input and you're back to that basic screen but it is no longer blank. It now carries all those facts you've entered.

Go through the same procedure for your spouse and, as always, don't forget to sign off with the Save button. That screen is filling up.

Now if you have children, go for the Male Child and Female Child buttons and you can put in the same Facts that have been entered for you and your wife.

Back to the screen and you'll see children boxes in that fence at the bottom. But their Facts will not be on display. No problem. Click on the child whose Facts you want to see and the screen will change to show that child in the main male or female position that you and your partner were in and the Facts on display.

You will be there in the parents box – click on it and you are back where you started.

You will notice that the PC has not asked you for your parents. Again, simple. Click on one of the empty boxes above you or your spouse, square for a father, rounded for a mother, and this puts them in the pole position and you are relegated to the child spot. You can now enter their Facts.

From these basic building blocks you can build up your entire pedigree. And the magic doesn't end there. You will have noticed that next to the Facts button there is a Notes button. Here you can type and store all sorts of information, usually up to several thousand words, on the individual concerned.

Close your eyes and imagine all of that spread over several generations and dozens of individuals and you will see the capacity of this amazing information system.

You can print out the material or copy to back-up disks at any time in case you have any worries about all your work disappearing one day as the result of some virus or gremlin or plain human error. But I'm panicking you. Don't worry: the PC is tenaciously possessive as far as your data is concerned. It won't surrender your efforts easily.

In addition, you can produce, from the information collected and stored, charts showing ancestors (pedigrees) or descendants (drop charts).

As usual with PC products, the software makes access to individual details very simple, either by clicking up or down the screens using the parents or children boxes or by searching for specific names.

There is always an array of additional facilities – calendars, relationship indicators and such like and, as the software is designed specifically for genealogical use, you can take for granted that it will accommodate all the variations that you can throw at it – illegitimate births, adopted children, marriages between kissing cousins, divorces, any number of step-children or re-marriages. Even if you do not have your own PC, there must be one in the family somewhere – and a relative who will be happy to install a package and help you key in your information. You will, of course, need to study carefully the instructions for whatever package you buy, but I hope these mouthwatering basics will convince you that no ancestor-hunter should be without a PC.

THREE

New Register House, Edinburgh/1

Births, Marriages and Deaths since 1855. How to find a great-great-great grandmother in a couple of hours.

At the Balmoral Hotel end of Princes Street, modestly peeping from behind the contrasting shoulders of a fast-food outlet and Register House, home of the National Archives of Scotland, lies New Register House, home of the General Register Office for Scotland (hereafter GRO). There, under one roof or perhaps dome to be more poetic, lies the most comprehensive collection of original genealogical source material to be found in Britain and maybe even anywhere outside Salt Lake City. In England, the equivalent information is dispersed throughout St Catherine's House, London, the Public Records Office, hundreds of parish churches and scores of local libraries, archives and repositories. Here, under that elegant neo-Georgian dome, the person in search of his Scottish roots can tuck into the records of every birth, marriage and death in Scotland since 1 January 1855, into the census lists of every person living in Scotland on the relevant day in 1841, 1861, 1881, 1891 and 1901, and into 4,000 volumes of old pre-1855 records from over 900 parishes.

Clearly this treasure-house is at the heart of any research you are likely to do. It takes up a correspondingly large part of this book, because it is difficult to conceive of any ancestor-hunter who will not rely heavily – indeed in some cases even exclusively – on the material housed in New Register House. There are some things you can profitably prepare before you get to the treasure dome.

NOTEPADS AT THE READY

The first thing that you can do at home in advance of your visit to New Register House is to prepare notebooks which you will use there. Again the question of note-taking is a very personal one – and you will see every type of notebook being used, from large and voluminous pads to tiny wallet-size ring books. One thing is certain – you must turn up with a substantial amount of paper to cope with the information.

I prefer the standard journalist/shorthand ring notebook. I start off with three – one for Births, one for Marriages and one for Deaths. This slight extravagance makes it possible to do, in advance, a lot of the chores which would otherwise take up valuable time in amongst the registers. Alternatively, you can divide the book into three – the first part for Births, the second for Marriages and the third for Deaths.

Better still, print off supplies of the family group sheet or individual sheet and carry these in ring-binders. You will then be putting your notes – in pencil at the GRO, as the use of pens is not permitted there – directly into the form to which they will eventually be transcribed – in ink – at home.

A BOOK AND A MAP

One final area in which you can get down to valuable work at home is swotting up the background. At this stage, you may not know exactly which part of Scotland you are going to be concentrating on, but as soon as the search becomes more localised it is important, especially in the rural areas, to get hold of a good Ordnance Survey map of the area. These often include names of old places, forgotten places, small places, which it would otherwise be difficult to relate to each other. It will also help you to track down addresses that you will be coming across in the records. In the case of the cities, a good street map would be helpful. While ideally an old map is to be preferred, it is surprising how many modern street maps of Scottish towns can prove helpful in locating nineteenth-century addresses.

The map or maps will provide you with valuable geographical information; you will also need some historical background as your search progresses. Here I have no hesitation in recommending a single book, Professor T C Smout's *A History of the Scottish People, 1560-1830,* a superb work on the people of Scotland, clearly describing the social context in which your ancestors lived, whether they were miners or lawyers, weavers or landowners, farmers or doctors. First-class illustrations and the rare combination of learning and style make this an ideal book for would-be ancestor-hunters, whether they are devoted addicts of historical writing or someone coming to the field as a novice. There will plenty of more specific books coming to your attention as your search becomes more focused.

HOW DO YOU GET STARTED?

The first step is to 'sign on' at the GRO. Be warned: you are not alone. Despite the significant investment in expanding the number of places for researchers – there are now one hundred 'work stations' – demand exceeds desks for a large part of the year. The queue forming outside New Register House before nine each morning is evidence of that fact.

You'll need to 'buy', in advance or on the day, a seat in one of the search areas. The booking procedure is quite straightforward and will be explained when you arrive.

You can book your seat for a day (£17 in 2001), a week (£65), four weeks (£220), a quarter (£500) or a year (£1,500).

Don't be daunted: the longer periods are of course aimed at the professional genealogists. It is unlikely that any individual would need such a lengthy commitment. There are some bargain (£10) one-day prices in the winter months, and even a part-day offer if there are empty seats after lunch.

When you've paid your money, you get your pass (you'll need to show it whenever you enter the building) and a seat number.

To be fair to researchers, the GRO offers a mix of seats which can be booked in advance and those which are kept for the folk in the morning queue. If you are travelling some distance it is well worth booking by phone in advance. See Appendix I for details.

Let's assume you've checked in, paid up and been taken to your seat.

You will be faced with a computer screen and keyboard (no mouse) and a microfiche reader. It is difficult to believe that this simple combination will unlock the full riches of civil records since 1855, church records before that period and the census returns of 1881 and 1891.

There are other groups of records kept at the GRO which are listed in Appendix II.

And you'll soon get to appreciate the well-stocked library shelves.

Let us start, as you almost certainly will, with those civil records.

From 1 January 1855, every birth, marriage and death that took place in Scotland had to be registered with the civil authorities. It was one small step in the new role of central and local government that came with the industrialisation of Britain.

New Register House is the home for the massive amount

of paperwork generated by this decision, nearly 145 years' worth of Births, Marriages and Deaths at your disposal!

Scotland had, by the standards of her neighbours, been surprisingly slow to introduce statutory civil registration. England and Wales had brought it in eighteen years earlier in 1837. Scottish ancestor-hunters have tutted ever since at this delay, especially unforgivable in a nation that had always prided itself on a sense of ancestry and the past. One compensation is that when the Scots did get around to civil registration, they did it with a thoroughness that has been the envy of those neighbours who made an earlier start.

In 1855, the exuberance was a little too uncontrolled and the certificates for that year contain an unequalled wealth of detail. This proved so difficult to maintain that all three categories (Births, Marriages and Deaths) were required to make less detailed returns from 1856 onwards. Even so, the material in Scotland without exception is much more genealogically useful than its equivalent south of the Border.

The death certificate provides a simple illustration of this. In England and Wales the certificate is of value only in providing an estimated age, an address and, as a matter of interest, the cause of death. The Scottish death certificate has the advantage of indicating whether or not the person was married and if so to whom, and even more significantly of naming the parents of the dead person – an essential pointer to an earlier generation missing in the London counterpart.

Before going on to look at the statutory records, I must re-emphasise the importance of collecting, at home, as many copies as possible of birth, marriage and death certificates held in the family. This will greatly increase your productivity at GRO.

THE INDEXES

The first point of contact with the records of civil registration is the collection of indexes. When the first edition of *Scottish Roots* was published, these were impossible to miss when you entered the public area beneath the fine dome, nearly one thousand volumes taking up sixty yards or so of shelf space, some of them weighing quite a bit. Genealogy was not only fun – it was slimming!

Today the indexes are all available on that computer screen in front of you, considerably speeding up the search.

Note: in one of the most dramatic moves of recent years, these indexes can for the first time be consulted at home via the web. I have dealt in detail with this in the 'Doing It From a Distance' chapter.

Using the keyboard, you type in the object of your search, names of the individual, sex (a legacy of the original indexes which were divided into Male and Female), event (birth, marriage or death) and year (precise or approximate).

The computer will search the indexes and offer you on screen one or more possible matches. A special point to bear in mind when consulting these indexes is that they refer to the year in which the event was registered and not the year in which it happened. In most cases, the two will be the same, but occasionally you will find an event appearing in the indexes the year after it took place. This is not only in obvious cases where end-of-the-year hatches, matches and despatches hang over from the December to the January, but also in a small number of cases when, after the normal period allowed for registration, evidence comes to light of, say, a birth which has not been registered. Defaulting parents would be reminded of their obligation and the entry duly made, and indexed for the point at which the information is registered. It is worth recalling that even someone as illustrious as Her Majesty the Queen Mother had an absentminded father who forgot to register her birth in the time allotted.

BIRTHS

Births offer the simplest of the indexes – you have no real choice. If you are looking up the birth of James Smith or Jane Smith, that is that. You have no alternative. When you have found the one you are looking for, note the registration district and the entry number. These are shown on the screen and, along with the year, are enough to identify precisely any birth registration.

You should realise that in the case of Births, Marriages and Deaths, unless you are absolutely sure that the entry you have tracked down is the right one (an unusual name, a precise date or a small registration district would help here) you should note down all possible entries to fall back on in case your first choice leads you to a dead end. When you eventually get up to see the entry and find that it's not your William Robertson, it is a good idea to have another likely individual at hand to follow up and that will save you a lot of time.

Where there is a middle name – a practice which came into fashion over the period we are talking about – this can often prove a help to sorting out your target from a host of contenders. You should not, however, assume that the absence of the middle name for which you are looking means that the person is not the right one. Often the name was added later in life and may appear on marriage or death certificates but not on birth certificates. Conversely, a name given at birth may disappear by the time a person marries or dies.

MARRIAGES

Here the format is very similar, but now of course you are actually looking for two people, so you have a choice of which one to go for. In fact, as the woman is listed by both maiden and married name, you have a choice of three. The choice enables you to avoid some of the problems associated with having a common name or combination of names to look up. Let us say you are looking for a marriage between William Robertson and Jane Alexander. All four names are fairly common in Scotland, so you would probably go for the Jane Alexander combination which will be a little bit easier. When you find a likely Jane Alexander entry, you can check that there is a corresponding Jane Robertson or William Robertson entry to match. This will confirm beyond reasonable doubt that you have the right pair

Be on the lookout for any way in which you can simplify your search. A particular warning is needed for the Mac names. In the indexes 'Mac' appears in a different spot from 'Mc', unlike the modern telephone directories which treat forms of the prefix as the same. If there was a clear distinction between the two forms, there would be no problem other than that of human error, but the modern concept of 'correct' spelling was certainly not widespread in the nineteenth century. Not only might the clerk who is filling in the form spell it differently from your forebear, that forebear himself might not have any standard way of doing it. In most cases, there was a cheerfully haphazard attitude to spelling. I have instances of an Alexander Macfarlane who signed his name with three different spellings in the four examples of his signature that I have found! The upshot of this type of inconsistency is that to be sure of checking a

Mac name you have to look up 'Mac' and 'Mc' separately in the indexes. That is very time-consuming, so if possible in marriages avoid the Mac partner, except for confirming an entry.

It is not only the surnames that can help – double Christian names or unusual Christian names can also help you track down someone with a common surname.

As in the case of Births, the correct entry in the index will give you a unique identification combination for a Marriage – year, registration district, entry number. This is all you need to locate the exact entry.

DEATHS

Once again, the female entries are listed twice – once under maiden name and once, when the woman was married, under her married name. This again reflects the Scottish recognition of the importance of a woman's independent name – and in the old days explained the excessively heavy Female indexes in Marriages and Deaths!

This gives you an option if you are looking up a female death. It will be much easier to find Ann Girdwood Miller under Ann Girdwood than Ann Miller

An even more useful innovation – relating to both males and females, married and single – came in 1868 when the death indexes included the age of the person involved. You will probably find for yourself the frustration of looking up lots of William Robertsons in the early death indexes only to find they are infants and certainly not the aged patriarch you are seeking. After 1868, the entry 'Robertson, William, 5' will tell you that he is not for you and the entry 'Robertson, William, 73' will raise your hopes. But remember these ages are often inaccurate, so don't rule out that

73-year-old Willie just because you know the one you are looking for would have been 76 in that year.

I have indicated the ways that are available to you to try and minimise the chores of hunting for people with common names. It is worth at this stage mentioning the other side of the coin – dealing with a family with an unusual name. If the name is a rare one, it may be worth your while making a note of all references to it in the indexes even if you do not at this stage intend to look at those registrations. In this way, you can identify previously unknown branches, or see certain patterns of names and geographical locations. When, for example, I was searching for members of my wife's family – Balbirnie – it was easy to identify a large clump of Tayside names, a smaller one in the West of Scotland and another in Edinburgh. The Christian name distribution was distinctive: Peter and David appeared only in Tayside, Charles and Henry only in the West, Robert and Alexander only in Edinburgh. When I came across a Robert, out of place in Glasgow, I followed it up – and found he had moved through from Edinburgh and was indeed one of ours.

This 'total' logging of index entries can only be justified when the name is truly unusual – and the indexes themselves will tell you whether or not that is the case.

FROM INDEXES TO ENTRIES

Having tracked down the relatives you are seeking, you have enough information to identify the exact entry in the Civil registers.

Make a note of the details on the small form supplied at each desk and your work is under way.

In theory, in order to find out what information is carried, you have to order a copy of that entry from the Registrar-

General, a procedure that can take a few days. There is naturally a charge made for this service, and current tariff is shown in Appendix I. The copy, incidentally, may take the form of either a direct photostat of the entry or the details typed onto a pro forma sheet.

This service is open to all, with the alternatives of being able to collect the copies or have them posted to you. It is quite expensive and, for genealogical purposes, a little slow, delaying the time at which you can make use of the information on the records to move forward to the next stage.

There is however another, more common alternative. The Registrar-General has for many years – and it is worth stressing, as James VI and I used to do to his Parliament, the privilege comes by grace and not by right – allowed people to inspect the entries on microfiche without addition to the original fee charged for inspecting the indexes.

This privilege is perhaps the most important single difference between England and Scotland as far as the genealogist is concerned. It cuts down the cost and time involved in building up a pedigree (family tree or chart), as well as allowing you to see the signatures or crosses of forebears and come to some assessment of how literate they may have been!

To look at the actual entry fill in the details and go off in search of the appropriate microfiche. At first you'll need to ask directions from the staff, but it won't take you long to get the hang of the place.

Take out the microfiche – for the inexperienced, a simple plastic 'postcard' carrying hundreds of photographic images – pop in your order form as a record of where the microfiche has gone and go back to your desk.

At first, you may need help to load and view the microfiche, but GRO staff are on hand – and they know that you'll soon get used to the manoeuvre.

The end result is that you should soon find yourself peering at a screen that shows the entry you are looking for.

This is where all that work you did at home drawing up the sheets of your notebook comes in helpful, for you have on your page all the headings which appear in the records and all the details you should record. That can sometimes prompt you into noticing that you've skipped a fact.

Incidentally, consider the time you have taken to get in front of this information and don't skimp on the notes. Items such as the name of the informant (the person giving the information to the registrar) may seem unimportant at the moment, but you never know when that fact may be of some value.

When you've finished, leave the microfiche in one of the filing baskets near your desk. Don't try and be helpful and file it away yourself.

The procedure is exactly the same for the records relating to Marriages and Deaths. You are allowed up to three microfiches at any one time and it is a good idea to try and take the full allowance. In the early stages in particular, it will not be possible to get three marriages or two deaths, as you may be looking for the information on one key entry to get you going.

So you've reached the stage of collecting details from the Births, Marriages and Deaths entries. What will the entries tell you – and what should you especially keep an eye out for? I shall deal with each of the categories in turn, showing what information is carried – and adding, just in case you strike the jackpot, just what bonuses await you if you land on one of those 1855 entries that carried so much extra material.

THE BIRTH CERTIFICATE

CHECK

First of all check the name of the person and any other detail you know which will confirm that you are in fact looking at the right entry. When you are sure this is really your man (or woman), make a note of the details as they appear.

AMENDMENTS

Pay particular attention to the first narrow column that is so easily overlooked and is rarely, if ever, mentioned in the books on genealogy. This shows whether or not an addition or amendment to the entry exists and if so gives you a reference number. Once an entry is made it cannot be altered – but it can be augmented. In the case of a birth certificate, for example, an additional name or a paternity action may be recorded elsewhere. If this is the case, that little first column will tell you. It doesn't crop up very often, but when it does it can provide valuable information. Ask one of the GRO staff to guide you to the supplementary entry.

THE NAMES

Take down all the names of the person as they may come in useful in establishing name patterns and relatives. Some of these names may well disappear later in life, but if they don't they will be useful in finding the right person in the indexes.

THE ADDRESS

Where and when born: unlike the English certificates, the time of birth is given in all cases. South of the Border, this distinction is reserved for twins and other multiple births. It is perhaps the only element of no genealogical significance, although astrologers may find it of interest. Note the address, as you may need it for Census leads.

PARENTS' DETAILS

Note name and profession of father (there may be a variation from any facts you already know); name and maiden name of mother (very important); the date and place of their wedding (a really significant item, yet another example of the value of Scottish records as opposed to those elsewhere in Britain).

One point worth making: don't be too surprised if the date turns out to be slightly inaccurate – this was before the widespread celebration of wedding anniversaries and many a spouse was less than precise when it came to this fact.

I have come across one Scot who gave a different date on each of the certificates of his four children – and not one of them agreed with the date in the parish records! This important detail – the date and place of the parents' marriage – was omitted from the certificates from 1856 to 1860, inclusive of both years. If your ancestor was born in this 'blank' period, it is worth checking up on his brothers and sisters born outside those years to get the information, as it will most likely refer to the pre-1855 period when you will need to know parish and date to stand any chance of success.

SIGNATURE OF INFORMANT

This also gives qualification/relationship and address if different from the one at which the birth took place: information which could be of value – make a note of it.

As you see, the typical birth certificate (there will be minor changes from one period to another) carries a wealth of information. Not least is the fact that it is the only certificate where the age of the person concerned (zero) can be guaranteed with any precision!

THE 1855 BONUS

In 1855, the entries included details of whether or not the birth took place in lodgings, the parents' ages and birthplaces, and other issue both living and deceased.

THE MARRIAGE CERTIFICATE

With two people involved, the marriage certificate is naturally the most heavily congested of the three as far as information is concerned. It is therefore especially important that you do not miss the details in the general *embarras de richesse*.

AMENDMENT

There is again a space to note any addition or amendment. I have not yet come across such an item but keep an eye out and ask for help if anything appears there. A reference there could refer not only to a clerical error but also to a divorce or, rarely, to a bigamous marriage.

THE WEDDING CEREMONY

Details include date, place (sometimes a church, sometimes the house of the bride – in any case make a note as it may come in handy later on), whether, in the case of marriages before 1 January 1978, performed after Banns or by licence, the Church according to whose forms it was performed. [Note: this may provide a useful guide to the Church the family attended, a valuable point when it comes to the pre-1855 searches.] You will also come across the 'irregular' marriages including the well-known 'Gretna Green' type. You will find a note on these in Appendix IV.

THE GROOM

Details of name, occupation, condition (bachelor, widower), age (a useful guide but never to be taken as gospel), address (handy for tracking down his family in Census returns), name and occupation of father; name and maiden name of mother. Take down all details, even when you think you have them from other sources – a man's description of his job, for example, may change slightly but significantly.

THE BRIDE

Similar details to those given for the groom, although it is not common to give occupation. As in the case of the man, the listing of the parents usually indicates when one or both of these is dead at the time of the marriage.

Generally speaking, if a parent is listed as 'deceased' this can be taken as proof; in the mere absence of the word 'deceased' you should not accept for certain that this is the case, as this is a not unknown oversight or omission.

THE WITNESSES

Do not neglect to record who signed the certificates. The names usually include the minister officiating (he can always be checked from directories if there seems to be some relationship indicated by the name), the best man/relative of the groom, and the bridesmaid/relative of the bride. Note them – they may be of some use.

REGISTRAR

There is rarely any point in making a note of this item.

THE 1855 BONUS

The 1855 goodies are, in the case of the Marriage certificates, less spectacular and more restricted than for the Birth and Death certificates. In that year, there was a distinction made between present and usual residence and both were stated and, in addition, details were given of any former marriages and the number of children, living and deceased, from these.

THE DEATH CERTIFICATE

As I hinted earlier, the Scottish certificate differs dramatically in its value to ancestor-seekers in comparison with the English record, which usually provides less than the barest gravestone. Look out for the following:

THAT LITTLE FIRST COLUMN

This will tell you if there was a Fatal Accident Enquiry and will even lead you to the findings of that enquiry. In the case of the death on 24 September 1884 of a seven-year-old girl, Margaret Mackay, I noticed a reference in that first column. Corrections 68512 Vol. VI, page 2, revealed that the head injuries referred to in the Death Certificate had been caused when the child, playing in one of those towering Edinburgh tenements while waiting for her tea, fell from the banisters and was killed. In some cases an incident such as this might lead you to a newspaper report.

NAME AND DETAILS OF PERSON

Again note the profession which is given and also details of any marriages. In the case of a married woman dying, the occupation of her husband is given.

WHERE DID THE DEATH OCCUR?

Here you are told not only the place of the actual death, but also the home address of the person concerned where this is different. In the case of death in hospital, for example, this is a valuable addition.

HOW OLD WAS THE PERSON?

Make a note of it, even although it may not be absolutely accurate.

PARENTS

The names of both parents are given, together with profession of father and maiden name of mother.

CAUSE OF DEATH

Even if the medical terms seem complex and irrelevant, try and get them down. The column will also tell you how long the disease had persisted and the name of the medical attendant. I've yet to find a really useful source to explain just what modern illnesses lay behind these unfathomable old terms. Any reader who knows of such a guide would do ancestor-hunters a service by sharing the information.

THE INFORMANT

Do not neglect this column which tells you who gave the information to the Registrar, in what capacity (usually a stated relationship to the deceased or, for example, landlord or neighbour where the person was living in rented property). These details are important for two distinct reasons.

First, they may help you establish other family relationships: when, for example, I saw from the death certificate of one James T B Alexander that the informant was a brother-in-law, Mr Ralph Linton, it told me that the deceased, who was not married to a Linton, had a sister who had at one stage married Mr Linton.

Secondly, by knowing who had furnished the information, you are more able to assess whether or not it is likely to be reliable in the difficult details. Despite the example of the certificate for the famous Scots Socialist, Keir Hardie, where his half-brother was clearly not aware of the fact that they were not full brothers, a person's brother can usually be trusted to provide the names of the parents with some precision; the keeper of a boarding house will be less reliable.

I have experienced instances where there is a discrepancy in the parentage given on two documents. A knowledge of the persons supplying the information allowed me to decide which was the more reliable. Subsequent information confirmed that approach.

THE 1855 BONUS

The extra 1855 details can, in the case of the Death Certificate, be enormous, spanning an incredible period of years. It gave in addition to the already full standard death certificate mentioned above: place of birth, details of marriage, burial place (a useful tip-off if there are tombstones still in existence) and a list of all issue living or deceased!

A specific example will give you some idea of just what is possible if you hit on the right person dying in 1855.

William Balbirnie, a copper engraver specialising in music printing, died 9 May 1855. We are told that he lived at 391 Lawnmarket, that he died of consumption and had been troubled by it for two years, that he was 56 years old (an accurate detail as it turns out – his 57th birthday would have come nine days later), that he had seven children with names, that he had been married to Catherine Johnstone, and that he was buried in the Old South Ground, Calton Cemetery. His parents were given as James Balbirnie, shoemaker, and Ann Dundas.

That is a considerable amount of information from a single document, accurate in nearly every detail. It included the name and occupation of a father who was born in 1760, and was provided by the deceased's son, who was to die in 1871 – a span of 111 years, on a single certificate.

The information in this case was precise: it was provided by a son who was a commercial clerk, used presumably to handling facts and figures and able to give details of his grandparents as they had in fact both died at advanced ages (80), so he must have known them well. The only detail he slipped up on was when, listing the children (his brothers and sisters), he had to include a sister who had died as a baby when he was only two years old. She had been christened 'Bethea' – he listed her as 'Bythnia'. A vessel of similar name was at that time involved in the Crimea activities and may have influenced his version!

This indicates the problem at the root of the high ambitions held by those who framed the first Scottish registrations: the ability to provide reliable details to fill in all those boxes depended so much on the informant. In our example, the informant was a son used to bookwork, who remembered his grandparents well. What if those grandparents had died before he was born? What if there was no relative to report the death?

By coincidence, one of William's sons died in hospital at around the same time. His death was reported by the supervisor of the hospital, who was not only unable to fill in many of the columns but also managed to spell the surname incorrectly – an error which delayed the finding of that particular entry. Searching for a BALbirnie, I could be excused for not finding a BILbirnie.

Hazards such as these were probably the reasons behind the discontinuing of the detailed records in 1856 – and might even mean that you could hit the jackpot (1855) and still be disappointed with a number of unanswered questions when you come to see the actual entry.

That completes a rundown of what you can expect to find in the post-1855 records of Births, Marriages and Deaths.

I shall outline in a similar manner what is contained in the other two great treasuries of information held by the GRO – the Censuses and the Old Parish Records (pre-1855). I shall then show, with actual case histories, just how these three can be combined to produce a fine scaffolding of family relationships on which to build your family history.

FOUR

New Register House, Edinburgh/2

The Census returns from 1841 to 1901. Where was your great-great granny on 31 March 1851?

In 1801, Britain made its first attempt to count the heads in the kingdom – and did it again in 1811, 1821 and 1831. These were of little value to the genealogist as we have, except in some rare cases, only the actual totals with no details of individuals. On 7 June 1841, Britain carried out the first door-to-door, person-to-person census for which we have the detailed enumerators' transcript books. These, carrying the name, occupation and approximate age of 2,620,184 people living in Scotland on that day, launched the second great source of raw material for the Scot in search of his roots.

As with civil registration, the Census has led many a researcher to sigh and ask why it had not been started much earlier.

The answer is perhaps a simple one. In the stable, even static society that characterised pre-industrial Britain, there was no obvious need for a census – and certainly not for a census with itemised individuals. There had been an attempt, as early as 1753, to instigate a national (i.e. British) census, but Parliament had rejected the proposals. A deciding factor in the rebuttal was the stance of the religious objectors. They found a clear warning at the end of Samuel's lengthy contribution to the Old Testament when 'David, tempted by Satan, forceth Joab to number the people' and, one might add, produceth some rather nasty manifestations of the Lord's anger. Not even that same Lord's apparent pleasure at a later tax-orientated census, making it the occasion for the birth of Christ, could make up for Samuel's clear warning that censuses were evil.

Nevertheless, the transformation of Britain brought about by the arrival of the machine and the factory saw a flight from the countryside to the towns, and the authorities decided that some attempts should be made to chart these changes. The Ordnance Survey was set up before the end of the eighteenth century as one way of doing this. The civil registration that we have looked at in the preceding section was another. In between these two came Britain's first census – in 1801. This, a strictly statistical exercise in which householders were numbered but not named, was the first of a series of regular ten-yearly censuses which have been held right up to the latest census year of 2001 – with the sole exception of 1941 when Britons had other things to worry about

It is worth emphasising at this point the particularly valuable contribution that the Census returns of 1841 and 1851 make to genealogical research in Scotland. While the Census was a British affair (as opposed to civil registration which was undertaken by the Scots, English, Welsh and Irish in different ways and at different times), it had an extra significance in Scotland.

Because Scottish civil registration did not take place until 1855, the Census returns contain information about people not covered by the statutory records. This is in distinct contrast to the state of affairs in England and Wales where civil (i.e. total) registration of Births, Marriages and Deaths had already been in place for four years *before* the first useful census (1841) took place. In Scotland, on the other hand, civil registration came into effect four years *after* the second (1851) census was set up. Clearly the returns of 1841 and 1851 will carry names and details of very many people not covered by the post-1855 records.

For this reason, the Census returns play a much more important part in Scottish genealogical investigation than is normally suggested in books written on a broader English-orientated basis.

So the enormous fund of information represented by the Census returns is at your disposal. Where is it? How do you 'plug in'? What will you find when you get hold of the material? The answers to those questions come rather in the form of a good news/bad news/good news story.

Good news

Once again the returns are stored in the same building as the statutory records – New Register House at the East end of Princes Street, Edinburgh. There are also good local returns held in local libraries.

Bad news

There was originally no indexing of the Census returns other than by town or village or, in the case of the cities, by street. That means that you have to know not the personal details of an individual (which were enough to lead you to the exact entry in the statutory records), but where he was living on the day that the census was taken. But don't be too perturbed – it is usually possible to answer, with some degree of accuracy, such questions as 'Where was your great-great granny on the evening of 31 March 1851?'

Good news

Indexes for the whole of Scotland have been compiled for the 1881, 1891 and 1901 Censuses which allow you to search by name. The index to the 1881 Census can in addition be bought from the Church of Jesus Christ of the Latter Day Saints (LDS) as a CD-ROM to enable you to search at home. You'll find more details in the 'Doing It from a Distance' chapter.

Local family history societies and others have also made a good stab at indexing their own areas for some of the earlier censuses, so you may well land up being able to bypass the 'address' entry system.

If you are interested in these later censuses, you can do the index search from your desk and get the microfiche in exactly the same way as the Births, Marriages and Deaths entries.

But let's assume for the moment that you are being led back to earlier censuses. After all, these are the ones most likely to take you back beyond 1855 to the Old Parochial Records (OPRs).

You will need to know an address to look for, because that, at present, is the only guaranteed 'open sesame' to the earlier censuses.

Your work on the Births, Marriages and Deaths records will have given you a number of events which provide addresses to try in the Census returns.

Obviously the nearer these events are to an actual census date, the better chance you stand of finding your ancestors in! In the case of city dwellers, the trade directories can sometimes provide an alternative means of finding an address near a census date – but bear in mind that such directories are usually prepared the year before the date shown on the cover. Let's take an example:

Having from a street directory discovered that Hugh

Dalrymple Alexander M.D. had his surgery at 46 Canongate and lived at 21 St John Street, Edinburgh, we go up to the South Search Room on the first floor of New Register House. There you can consult indexes for each Census indicating which areas are covered by which microfilm.

You look up St John Street in the Edinburgh 1851 Census Street Index. We find that the street is in Census District 685-3 and is covered in enumerators' books 75 and 76. We look for the microfilm containing books 75 and 76 and we work our way through the pages looking at the address column for St John Street. When we find it, we look for number 21. The numbers, especially of main roads, are not always in sequence as they follow the order in which the enumerator visited the houses and that may have involved leaving the road and covering alleys or side streets. This time, we have a short and straightforward street and soon find the entry. It reads as follows:

1. Hugh D Alexander, head of household, married, age 33, Physician, Surgeon M.D. St Andrews, Glasgow, General Practitioner, born Dumfries.
2. Jessie Alexander, age 32, wife, born Midlothian, Edinburgh.
3. Mary Alexander, daughter, age 7, born Midlothian, Edinburgh.
4. William Alexander, son, age 6, born Midlothian, Edinburgh.
5. Jessie Alexander, daughter, age 5, born Midlothian, Edinburgh.
6. Agnes Alexander, daughter, age 3, born Midlothian, Edinburgh.
7. Hugh Alexander, son, age 2, born Midlothian, Edinburgh.

8 John Alexander, son, age 6 months, born Midlothian, Edinburgh.
9 Denham S Kerr Alexander, brother, age 21, 4th year medical student, born Dumfries.
10 Margaret King, servant, unmarried, age 19, born Ireland.
11 Mary Lee, domestic servant, unmarried, age 19, born Edinburgh.

This gives us a very wide variety of genealogical information, notably the birthplace of Dr Alexander, the names and approximate birth dates of his wife, three daughters and three sons, and family information – that he was a physician and surgeon and had obtained his degree in St Andrews. In addition, we get the bonus fact that his brother, Denham Kerr Alexander, is following in his footsteps, but this time at the University of Edinburgh. The existence of two servants tells us something of the family's social standing.

The entry has delivered a complete family group in far less time than would have been possible using the Births, Marriages and Deaths approach. No less importantly, it has given us the pointers to take us back well beyond the 1855 frontier. We are, for example, to look for Dr Alexander's birth certificate in one of the Dumfries parishes in the year 1817 or 1818.

In this simple, but real, example, the Census returns have expanded a single-line entry in a trade directory into a family group of nine individuals. There is naturally an element of luck involved. In that example, we found what turned out to be the entire family still living with their parents. Ten years later, one or two might have flown the nest.

Another aspect of the luck element is that it is not

always possible to find the people you are looking for at home on the night of the census. While this would be more likely to apply to say a sailor than a shoemaker, a commercial traveller than a grocer, it is worth remembering that, at the time we are talking about, travel was still a slow business. Visits to relatives or business trips of what we would today consider to be short distances could, in those days, take people away from home for lengthy periods.

I have had several examples of bad luck of this sort, but had it all repaid when I had one stroke of good fortune.

A census was held on the day of a particular person's funeral and that enabled me to discover, staying the night, a knot of country cousins I would never otherwise have traced! The other side of that coin was that anyone looking for those country cousins at their end would have found an empty house.

WHAT DO THE CENSUSES TELL US?

Censuses were not established to help people build up a family tree or write a family history. They were set up by central government to provide it with certain information that it felt it needed to have. That information changed as circumstances changed and today we have a much more comprehensive and sophisticated census, with selected samples providing more detailed information than could ever have been imagined by the 1841 authorities. In each census, what you are in fact going to be looking at are the enumerators' transcripts from their original forms on to printed books. The legibility of the writing and the permanence of the ink vary considerably and the feature of checking through a long street is the way in which these change. With one book you are delighted with a bold black script – at the next you are struggling with a spidery sepia hand. The material is rarely if ever totally incomprehensible – and the staff will lend a friendly hand if you are really stuck.

The 1841 Census took place on 7 June 1841 and its main importance lies in the fact that it provides early information some fourteen years before Scotland's civil registration. The enumerators were given forms to fill in and their returns were to give the following information:

1 The address of the dwelling house.
2 The name of the individual.
3 The age of the individual (rounded down on the nearest 5).
4 The status, profession or occupation.
5 The answer to the question 'whether born in the county or not'.
6 Whether or not the individual is foreign.

The fact that the Government of the time was concerned primarily with the movement of people in this age of social upheaval is underlined by the questions relating to origin. The genealogist will bemoan the fact that he is not told the relationship of individuals to one another (although it is usually possible to guess with some degree of accuracy) or the exact age of the people (which would simplify later investigations of the Old Parochial Registers).

The 1851 Census was held on 31 March 1851 and marked a great step forward on three distinct fronts:

1 The relationship to the head of the household was indicated (together with the 'condition' of the person concerned – married, unmarried, widowed).
2 The age was given accurately – although it is worth

noting that the accuracy which was intended was not always achieved. Women in particular rarely seemed to age ten years between the decennial censuses – my own record is finding one who aged only three years between the 1851 and 1861 Census. The ages are naturally reasonably accurate in the lower ranges.

3 The place of birth is given in much greater detail, often down to the exact parish which is a great help when we come to look at the Old Parochial Registers.

Each census seems to have had its own little idiosyncrasy that can, in an admittedly limited number of cases, throw extra light on the family. In the case of the 1851 Census, there is a question asking whether the individual is blind or deaf-and-dumb. This perhaps represents the establishment's concern with social matters.

The 1861 Census was held on 8 April 1861 and was the first to be held after the introduction of statutory records in Scotland. This means that it deals only with those people who can be found also in the civil registrations. Its value would therefore seem to be limited to the sort of shortcut role indicated in our earlier example. It does, however, have the benefit of including a new question – indicating a further concern for social matters – namely, how many of the rooms occupied by the family contain one or more windows? It also frequently indicates whether the person was an employer and, when he was, how many people he employed.

These details help the researcher to learn something of the living conditions and financial position of his ancestors, an aspect which would not really emerge from the Births, Marriages and Deaths records.

Subsequent censuses, held on 3 April 1871, 4 April 1881, 5 April 1891 and 30 March 1901, follow very closely the now established format and the only really different information you are likely to discover comes with the latter censuses which indicate whether or not an individual speaks Gaelic. Again this would apply in only a minority of instances but where it is applicable offers a fascinating little sidelight.

When the 1901 Census came into the public domain, in early 2002, it was fully indexed, and the entries were available in digital form. This will give superb screen quality and will let you to select and zoom areas where you may have some problems reading the details.

I have concentrated on the role of the Census returns in combining with the statutory records and, as we shall see in the next chapter, with the Old Parochial Registers, together with the additional role of supplying those extras about disabilities, housing, Gaelic-speaking etc. There is another small way in which they can offer facts which are not given elsewhere – and that is in telling you something of what the females did. In many of the marriage records, we are not told what the bride did for a living, although the groom's occupation is nearly always supplied. The Censuses, taken in the family home *before* the marriage, will often tell you just what job the girl had [if any] and sometimes in quite useful detail. Such examples as 'straw-bonnet maker', 'shop assistant in draper's' or 'works in tobacconist shop' all surely add something of a knowledge of the person who is otherwise going to become little more than a wife-and-mother statistic.

By far the greatest value of the Censuses lies, to my mind, in their ability to fit a person or a family into an environment. Whenever I am taking down details about a family from the Census returns, I invariably make a note of the neighbours or, in a small village, of a wider spread of the community. I want to know just what sort of people lived nearby or what families dominated the village or, in the towns, who shared the same front door.

Surely part of the story of any family is not just who they were, when they flourished and what they did. I know much more of one of my wife's ancestors when I learn that he lived in the same building as a groom, a telephone engineer, a blacksmith, a newspaper office clerk, a brass founder and an animal portrait painter – and that just below him dwelt an Irish police constable and his wife, together with a mother-in-law and five working brothers-in-law!

Sometimes the Census returns can give you the flavour of a period or a place in a way that cannot be matched by the history books. The returns for 25 Carrubbers Close, Edinburgh, for example, show that in 1841 that crowded alley, which today forms a back lane for one of the capital's most respectable hotels, housed an unbelievable congestion of trades crammed into the 41 flats that shared the stair of number 25. Amongst the many shoemakers and tailors, glaziers and jewellers, cow-feeders and boot-closers jostled a large number of FS (female servants). Their presence is perhaps explained by the final entry of a husband and wife declaring themselves to be 'fleshers' (butchers). The supervisor of the enumerator has deleted the word 'flesher' and inserted in red ink 'brothel keeper'.

The history books and social history studies may give you the story of the country, the contemporary newspapers may relate that to an area or a city, but only the Census returns can take you down to the details of a village, a street or even a house.

FIVE

New Register House, Edinburgh/3

Parish records – back beyond 1855, where Births, Marriages and Deaths turn into Baptisms, Banns and Burials.

Leafing through the records of baptisms in the ancient Canongate records which include in their earliest marriages that of Mary, Queen of Scots, and Darnley, I came to an abrupt halt. There was an entry crossed out! I could understand a marriage entry being erased at the last moment and possibly, thanks to a brisk, reviving Scottish breeze, even a burial entry, but a birth entry?

I could not avoid reading through it, rather as the jury always seems to perk up and pay attention when the judge orders a particular testimony to be 'struck from the records'. The baptism seemed quite normal if a little bit upmarket. A Scottish aristocrat and his lady, with some impressive kinsfolk as witnesses, were playing their part in recording a perhaps long-awaited heir. But the whole entry was scored out and in the margin was written:

'His Lordship refused to pay the clerk his fee and this entry is accordingly razed out'!

That example underlines the one basic truth about the pre-1855 records: they were certainly not, nor were they intended to be, total and comprehensive. They had for many decades before 1855 meant paying out a sum of money, and the noble Earl referred to above, presumably able, despite the image of the eternally impoverished Scottish aristocracy, to afford the odd bawbee, was not alone in not thinking the operation worth the money. The recording, incidentally, was separate from the baptismal activity which appears to have gone ahead undisturbed.

Governments had at various stages imposed stamp payments on such entries and these, as with all taxes, had an immediate effect of a deterrent, an effect which may or may not have worn off as time went by. The records for Kirkcaldy at the end of the eighteenth century bewail one newly introduced payment and gave it as the reason for a sharp drop in the number of entries.

This is a far cry from the post-1855 situation where the state took on full responsibility for ensuring total registration.

In three other respects, the Old Parochial Registers show marked and, for the ancestor-hunter, frustrating differences from the newer records.

Firstly, there was no standard to which clerks were expected to conform. The result is that the information varies considerably from year to year, from parish to parish (as indeed does the quality of writing and degree of preservation).

Secondly, as these were church registers, they set out to record not so much births as baptisms (although the birth date was often given), not so much marriages as banns, not so much deaths as burials.

The third and greatest difference lies in the fact that civil registration brought with it in 1855 a responsibility for the care, preservation, storing and indexing of the records. Before 1855, this was a matter of individual practice and bent. This is reflected in the lists of OPRs held by the Registrar-General. Many parishes are defective in certain years, ranging from enormous gaps of decades at a time to small periods. Some parishes have little or no representation at all. Scotland has done much to preserve these records, to maintain them in a single building, and to make them available to the public. For over a century the actual original documents were available to researchers, but constant and increasing use threatened the old records and impaired their legibility. That is why you will be looking at microfilm and not originals.

Just how useful these records will be to you depends, however, not on the care and attention given to the documents today, but on that lavished on them before 1855 plus a great element of luck as far as survival is concerned.

Once again, you will want to know just how do you plug into this vast hoard of 4,000 volumes of handwritten registers from almost a thousand Scottish parishes, ranging in age from the baptisms and banns in the parish of Errol in Perthshire in 1553 to the registers compiled on the eve of 1855, when the responsibility passed to the state?

The first thing to understand, as far as the 'plugging-in' operation is concerned, is that the rules have changed yet again. In the case of the statutory civil registers, the 'unit' was the individual – let's say, William Forbes Miller. In the case of the Census returns, the 'unit' was an address – let's say, Sauchiehall Street, Glasgow or Cumbernauld Village. Now, in the case of the OPRs, the 'unit' is the parish. Without that information, there is no way into the records which will lead you to the person or family you are after. To know the name of a person and not the parish is like trying to find the telephone number of someone when you only know his Christian name.

By this stage you will have had some idea of which parish you are going to be playing in:

1 The Census returns from 1851 onwards included a note of the place in which the individual was born. In some cases this would have been given as the parish itself, in others perhaps the name of a large town or city, or even

(and you are going to curse your forebears for being so lazy) only the county.

2 The Births, Marriages and Deaths in the years immediately after 1855 will have given you some clue to the places in which a family lived.

3 You may even have had detailed information from the Bonus Year entries of 1855.

No matter what the state of play, you have to come to some conclusion about the parishes to be searched. If you have no idea of where to look at this stage, you must take steps to identify some of the later Census returns in order to find the information. If, for example, you were unable to find anyone at the address on an 1857 certificate when the Census was taken in 1861, you must try and find the birth of a brother or sister nearer the census year to help you find the new address. If you have only the details of the 1841 Census, which did *not* give place of birth, go and see if there was anyone at that address for the 1851 Census, which did.

If the worst comes to the worst, you will have to gamble. If the family were all living in Lanark in the 1850s, then try there for the births. The other facts which you will have noted from the Census returns and from such documents as the Marriage and Death Certificates will have been the approximate ages, and this information combined with the possible parishes will enable you to begin your search.

Once again, the first line into the OPRs is to be found at your fingertips at the GRO desk. Originally, these OPRs were unindexed. If you were lucky, you might find that the clerk kept a rough running index, grouping all 'As' in one section, all 'Bs' on another page. Names will not be in strict alphabetical order but easier to check than listing by date.

Some kind soul might have produced a fine typescript index, generally but not always in the larger towns, and if you were very, very lucky you will find there is actually a fully comprehensive published index.

Now the entire OPRs have been indexed with the same procedures as when you were looking at the state records. The main difference comes when you get to look at specific entries. The OPRs are kept not on microfiche but on microfilm, a palm-size cotton-reel device that needs a different type of reader from the one on your desk. You go off to the great dome to find and read the microfilm. There are a number of microfilm-reading machines there. Find an empty one and feed in the film. Again, you may need advice at first but it will soon all fall into place.

BIRTHS BECOME BAPTISMS

These were invariably the record of an actual baptism in the church – and as we are talking about records from the Church of Scotland, this limits us to members of that Church, although the various Presbyterian splinters were usually included with the mainline Church.

Aside from the basic problem of OPRs (sheer survival), we have the additional one of not every birth being accommodated by a baptism, although pressures, religious and social, did their best to see that it was. Sometimes a shortage of ready cash would defer, perhaps indefinitely, the religious ceremony. Sometimes you will find out that four or five brothers and sisters are baptised at once, the arrival of the latest baby providing the occasion for getting them all done. You can see what this will do to your searches if you are looking for a baptismal entry for William Miller whom you know to have been born in 1850/1, when in fact he was baptised along with three little Millers in 1854! Perhaps a new minister came in and decided to have a baptism drive.

Generally speaking, I get the impression that the pressures to get the child baptised were stronger on a family in a tightly knit rural community than on a family in one of the teeming urban centres.

The information given does not vary to any great extent. The name of the father and the mother invariably appears, usually with the mother's maiden name, the date of the birth as well as the baptism is stated and, in the earlier years, a particularly important feature is the listing of witnesses, generally two, one for each side of the family. In view of the sparse nature of information in the OPRs generally, these names can often provide confirmation of a relationship or reveal the existence of other members of the family. A typical combination of witnesses might be brothers of husband and of wife, fathers of husband and of wife.

They are usually furnished with some details about their occupations and location. A man may be described as a 'farmer of such and such a farm', or 'merchant in such a port'.

A feature in the birth entries which should be brought to the attention of any susceptible reader is the preoccupation, especially in the more rustic areas, with legitimacy. Where necessary, the phrase 'born in fornication' is used without hesitation and, in contrast to later registrations, the name of the erring father is invariably given. You must remember that basically we are dealing with the records of the Church in a community, and the moral role is one which plays a part even in the chronicling of births.

The occasional oddity will come up in these birth records. The existence of foundlings was widespread and the task of naming the child and integrating him/her into the community lay with the Church. The birth records reflect this concern. Great care is taken with naming systems. Readers of *Oliver Twist* will remember that he was called 'Twist' because they had reached 'T' in the alphabet. Many were given the name 'Kirk' or 'Church' if they were abandoned in the porch of the church. Others even had Christian names pinned to their clothes when found. Gerald Hamilton-Edwards in his excellent *In Search of Scottish Ancestry* gives the example of the foundling at Coupar Angus who was promptly named 'Angus Coupar'.

For all the colourful nature of this type of entry, it will invariably mean the end of one line as far as the genealogist is concerned. But don't forget in the case of illegitimate births to check out the Kirk Session records. The elders may well have hauled the erring father before them to explain his actions, even if this was many months later.

Sometimes you will find a clue to the naming of the legitimate offspring. In Dundee, one clerk instigated an efficient columnar system which simplified the recording of baptisms and included a column heading 'After whom the child is named'. In view of the rigid naming patterns of Scottish families (see Appendix III), this is an invaluable extra.

In other cases, the entry itself will enlighten you. For example, I was puzzled at the existence of a Walker Dundas in a family which had never used the name before, and where there was no evidence of its being brought in from the mother's side. When I found the actual baptismal entry for 22 April 1759, I saw that the witnesses included a Mr Walker, surgeon. Here was an example of another quaint custom of naming the child after the doctor, when it was his first delivery or when there was particular reason to thank him – for a difficult birth, perhaps. There was also a custom of incorporating the name of the minister if this was his first baptism.

MARRIAGES BECOME BANNS

In the cases of marriages, the rigid distinction between Church of Scotland and the other Churches was blurred. The reading of banns had a social as well as a religious significance and it was not uncommon to find the established Church mixing the functions. Banns relating to a Catholic couple could easily be read in a Protestant church and even a note made of the actual marriage taking place before a Roman Catholic priest. For the most part, however, we are again talking about the national Church's religious ceremonies rather than the systematic maintenance of a society's records.

The great pressure on the marriage being recorded was an obvious one – and goes some way to explaining that you will often come across families whose marriages have been religiously (in all senses of the word) recorded, but where there are no traces of any baptismal records. In pre-1855 communities, the Church's concern with morals focused very sharply on sexual morals. After all, Lust is the most apparent of the Seven Deadly Sins as far as its results are concerned! One can argue about Sloth and Envy, Pride and even Gluttony, but Lust usually comes to light more indisputably. And the only evidence you could produce in your defence was the marriage lines. Look at the records of the Sessions and you will find, time and time again, the deacons insisting on seeing the marriage lines as proof that there was no sin.

The information given in the records of banns and marriages is disappointingly slight. Sometimes you will find little more than the name of the two partners. When it is necessary to name parents, you will find this is usually restricted to the father of the bride. While this is a useful pointer to the next stage – an extra lug on the jigsaw piece in the case of the wife – the absence of this information in the case of the husband means that the only link with the earlier generation is through the birth/baptismal entry.

DEATHS BECOME BURIALS

If the records of births and marriages are far from satisfactory, the situation when it comes to deaths is even more likely to cause frustration. These records are basically not religious records in the sense that baptisms and banns are. They are records kept by the people who run the graveyards – usually in earlier times the responsibility of the church, but often, especially later in the period, people charged specifically with looking after the large urban graveyards.

Sometimes you have to rely on records which are not of interments but accounts of people borrowing the mort-cloth used in the ceremony. Even where records are well kept, the variation from one graveyard to the next is extraordinary

Take these two examples from Edinburgh graveyards which are actually within sight of each other. The entries were made in the same decade and refer, I think, to two brothers.

In the first case, the details, beside being splendidly written, include the name of the father, his occupation and address, the age of the person who has died, the cause of death and full details of the location of the grave. The information allowed me to fit the child confidently into the family history.

In the second case, the only information given is the

name of the person who has died and the date of the interment. Only the unusual name and the fact that I have records of the birth and apprenticeship of a James Balbirnie in 1783 and 1799 give me any defence for tentatively putting this down as the date of death of the person in my records. There is rarely if ever a mention of parentage in the case of the burial of an adult as opposed to that of a child.

Often the gravestones give more information than the written records. Indeed in many cases there are no written records. The logging of the grave inscriptions is therefore an important dimension to the maintaining of Scotland's records. This has been painstakingly undertaken by a number of Scotland's genealogists, notably by Mr John Fowler Mitchell and his wife, Sheila. The focal point for the work has become the Scottish Genealogy Society, publishing many lists and photocopying many more. As a result of the Society's work, there is a very good chance that some of the graveyards you are interested in have been logged. The 'stone books' can augment the paper documents and you'll find they cover not just those inscriptions relating to the high and powerful. Many Scots stretched their limited finances in order to pay for a good headstone.

A superb collection of these transcripts from the length and breadth of Scotland is available for study in the library of the Scottish Genealogy Society in Victoria Street, just off the Royal Mile below Edinburgh Castle. New Register House carries many of these in its own library.

The value of these transcripts lies not only in sparing you a trip to Inverness, either by showing what is on the family tomb or by telling you there isn't one there, but also in recording many inscriptions which are succumbing day by day to pollution and Scotland's high and acidic rainfall.

The OPRs are erratic, frustrating, difficult, and at times

the writing can be positively mind-boggling. For all that, they provide, through the occasional flash of an entry, an enormous amount of satisfaction. Perhaps they don't provide the wealth of data which comes from the post-1855 variety, but there is something more than a fact when you read, for example, in the quaintly penned records of Cramond Church that two forebears in 1732, 'James Dundass, baxter, and Elizabeth Cleghorn, daughter of the deceased William Cleghorn, tenant in Granton, gave a crown to the poor in pledge of marriage'.

SIX

The PC Owner's Super-Bonus

The Mormon files are online and can dramatically augment the information gathered at New Register House.

Of all the bonuses which ancestor-hunters will find on their PCs, none can compare with the availability of the massive databases of the Church of Jesus Christ of the Latter Day Saints (LDS), more usually referred to as the Mormons.

At www.familysearch.org, you can access, no matter where you live, parts of the largest collection of genealogical material in the world – and for just the cost of a local telephone call.

The site has many useful and fascinating corners, from background information on the Mormons and details of their libraries around the world, to useful tips on family research – after all they are the tops at this hobby. You can also order publications and CD-ROMs. But the greatest miracle of all comes when you click on SEARCH.

The screen will then offer you a deceptively simple array of a dozen or so boxes.

These will allow you to check with the Church's International Genealogical Index (IGI) to see if it holds details of any of your ancestors, found or as yet undiscovered.

The vast majority of the entries on IGI date from earlier than the civil records of post-1855.

The main pair of boxes relates to an individual, first name and family name. (For the most part forget middle names except in special circumstances which the guidance notes will explain.)

You can if you wish, or are able, include names of a spouse and parents.

You should now specify which event you are looking for: birth/christening, marriage, death. (Be warned the IGI is poor on deaths.) You can ask for all these events.

You may now specify a year and a year range – exact, plus or minus 2, 5 or 20.

Again you may ignore the year and the range.

Finally, you can specify a country and occasionally a state or region from the drop-down list. For the most part we are talking Scotland, but if you know great-great-uncle Hector went off to Sarawak, give it whirl.

There is a facility to specify the exact spelling of a name, but this is rarely productive and does expose you to the vagaries of ancestors, clerks and transcribers. It should be avoided.

Press Search and the computer will do just that, beavering through the millions of names held on IGI.

If successful, the Index will deliver an ancestor or, more likely, a list of matches for the names, event and place. These should help you narrow down the possibilities and by clicking on any likely names you can get further details to confirm or otherwise the individual concerned.

If you are looking for a common name, you may be faced with a lengthy choice. The system will not offer you more than 25, but there are ways of expanding this.

You will of course be able to narrow down the alternatives by being more specific. You'll have problems looking for the birth, marriage or death of a Gordon Macrae at an unspecified date, which will reduce greatly if you search instead for his marriage two years either side of 1822.

There is one final *coup de grace* to reveal. You can type in just the father and mother and leave every other box blank. The Search instruction will then produce a list of all the offspring of such a combination culled from the worldwide database.

This again will not really deliver if you are looking for a combination of quite common names. With so many to chose from and such a small percentage of the results to be displayed it would take a rare stroke of luck to see your target on the list.

But the slightest oddity in naming would greatly improve your chances. I have a specific example.

I had by a lengthy process established the parents of a Catherine Johnstone as being George Johnstone and Bethia Hall, but, as I had been unable to track down her birth/ baptism record in Edinburgh, this was unconfirmed by any document. (To show the sort of detective work you are likely to get involved in, I had established these parents on the basis that two of Catherine's seven children were named 'George' and 'Bethia', names which did not come from her husband's side. There were records of the births of two Johnstone children around 1800 with parents George and Bethia. I assumed Catherine was a sister and pencilled in the parents. Later, looking at graveyard records, I discovered she was buried with George and Bethia. I inked in the parents, but I still had no documentary evidence.)

When I first came across the IGI two-parent option, I decided that the inked-in mother's name was unusual enough to give it a try. I typed in George Johnstone and Bethia Hall and within seconds the screen offered, from the entire global database, just three Johnstone children, the two I had already traced – and Catherine. I had been searching the Edinburgh records where her siblings had been baptised, but she had been born in Musselburgh, only just outside the city boundaries. Bingo.

I mentioned earlier that most entries are pre-1855. They

should not be assumed to represent complete coverage of the Scottish OPRs. In some cases, you will find they have names you have not discovered in your work on the OPRs; in others, you will find the opposite and that you have unearthed individuals not listed on IGI.

Here is an example to quantify the differences. My own research had identified seven children of James Balbirnie and Ann Dundas. The IGI delivered the three daughters, but missed the four sons, even although they were born in the same parish and alternated with their sisters as far as births were concerned.

The good news hasn't ended yet. While the bulk of the data on offer is the IGI, it also includes substantial material from other people's ancestral files and relevant websites. It is almost impossible to hazard a guess at what this might mean to your individual searches but you will see an example of its impact on one family tree.

While IGI can deliver invaluable names, dates and places, it will also in most instances lead you directly to the entry in the OPRs or indeed the early civil records. Why, I hear you ask, do I need the originals? The answer is that sometimes you don't: the IGI gives you all that you are likely to find there. But in many instances, the extra information carried in the OPRs might be just what you are looking for. You may find a witness at a baptism or sometimes a parent or two at a marriage that the IGI has missed. It is up to you to decide whether or not a particular line from IGI merits a follow-up by a visit to GRO or indeed ordering a copy of the original.

SEVEN

A Spell at New Register House

Two case histories show how to combine the three great repositories for YOUR family research.

After listening patiently to a catalogue of the work I had done on my wife's family tree, a friend asked the simple question: 'How long did it take you to put all of this together?' I was hurtled into a well-oiled answer, emphasising the ease of the chase, the glories of the Scottish records and the spontaneity of my own deductions, before I came to an abrupt halt. I realised that I was committing what seems to be a prevalent sin among ancestor-hunters and in particular writers on the subject: I was forgetting the realities of the timescales in my enthusiasm for the end result. Look at any book on genealogy and you will see just what I mean: the writer condenses twenty years' search into a single book and forgets the months of search which were rewarded with but a single name or date, the days poring over records, the undergrowth of dead ends.

The lesson stuck and when, soon afterwards, I came to write a series of articles for The Royal Bank of Scotland's staff publication which was to lead to this book, I determined to avoid this pitfall. I looked for two willing guinea pigs who would, from a base of only a small amount of information on their forebears, set off on the search.

The project was to be confined to a token week examining records kept at New Register House (the statutory civil records since 1855, the Census returns and the Old Parochial Registers) because this represents a fund of information which will be applicable to nearly every searcher, because the methods would again be relevant not only to the two people but also to the readers of the article, and because the 'scaffolding' built up from these records is essential to any real success in the wider records of Scotland.

The two 'volunteers' were Pauline Brydon and Bob Leitch. Originally, I thought to cover the east and west coasts, as Pauline had been brought up on the south edge of Edinburgh and Bob to the south of Glasgow. As things turned out, within a generation we were back to Edinburgh in both cases! I owe a lot to both of them for their very willing co-operation in the search and their permission to use our findings in this book.

The studies were both carried out before New Register House had added computers and full microfiche facilities to its armoury, a move which would have speeded up the search. The principles of the search, however, remain exactly the same.

CASE HISTORY ONE

Pauline Brydon is extremely methodical and produces as our starting point the death certificate of her grandfather, James Brydon, originally obtained for insurance purposes.

This tells us that James, a retired stevedore, had been married to Margaret Reynolds and had died on 27 March 1969. His deceased parents are given as James Bryden, carter, and Margaret Bryden, m.s. (maiden surname) Stewart. It also indicates that the spelling of the name had changed from *Bryden* (his father's name) to Brydon. This is a symptom of the modern bureaucratic concern for standardised spelling which had little or no equivalent in the nineteenth century. We shall indeed find that his father had earlier been known as *Brydon* which brings us right back to where we started – and gives an early reminder of the problems of spelling in our work! A further note added that he had been born on 17 March 1894.

The two pieces of paper enabled Pauline to produce this rough chart immediately:

James Brydon m. **Margaret Stewart**
carter

|

James Brydon m. **Margaret Taylor**
stevedore
b. 17 March 1894
d. 27 May 1969

If she had not been able to lay her hands on that death certificate, we would have had to get that same information from the original held at New Register House.

We have a choice of tactics: we can either look for the birth certificate of the grandfather in order to find the date of his parents' marriage or we can try and bypass that stage by looking directly for the marriage. This is always a case of personal judgement, but here we have a fairly distinctive combination of names as far as the parents are concerned, so we try to find their marriage directly from the indexes.

This is a bit of a gamble especially when you realise that marriages in Scotland between 1861 and 1871 produced on average 4.5 legitimate births, and that if you have caught the tail end of a large family you could have a long backward trek to the original marriage. But here we risk it, encouraged perhaps by the fact that the son bears the same name as his father and is likely to be the first male offspring.

We are looking for the marriage certificate of James Bryden and Margaret Stewart. We pick one of the pair, James Bryden, on the grounds that there would be fewer James Brydens than Margaret Stewarts in the records. Looking at the Marriage Indexes, Males for 1893, we draw a blank; 1892, a blank; 1891, a blank; 1890, eureka! – a marriage entry for James Bryden, at the registration district of South Leith, entry number 118. We carry out a check. If he is our man, then there must be a corresponding entry for Margaret Stewart. So we check the 1890 index for female marriages and find Margaret Stewart, also South Leith 118. It looks as if we have the right pair.

On the marriage entry, the basic details are: James Brydon was a carter, aged 21, who lived at 13 Gordon Street, Leith (the port of Edinburgh) and his parents were William Brydon and Jennet Brydon, m.s. MacQueen. His bride was Margaret Stewart, aged 21, who lived around the corner from him at 24 Ferrier Street. Her parents were Thomas Stewart, boilermaker, and Janet Stewart, m.s. Morris.

This document enables Pauline to progress another generation and to add to her chart the following lines:

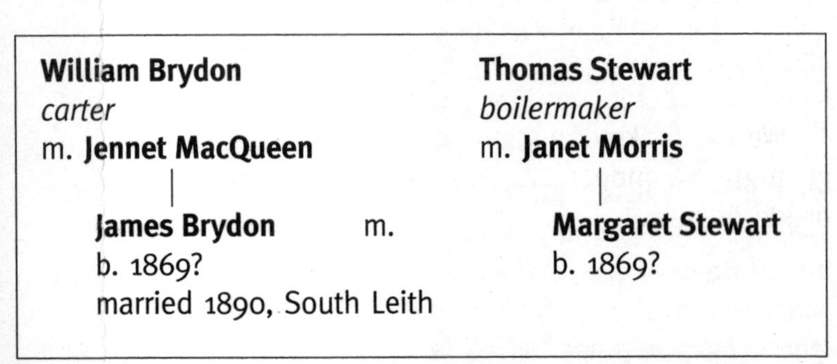

Eventually, we find, after a long time peering at the Name columns: Brydon, Book 25, Entry 75. It reads:

1 Margaret Brydon, widow, head of family, 31 years old.

2 William Brydon, son, aged 13, scholar.

3 Thomas, son, aged 11, scholar.

4 Margaret, daughter, 11, scholar.

5 Janet, daughter, 9, scholar.

6 James, son, 5, scholar.

7 Euphemia, daughter, 2.

All are shown to have been born in the same area (Leith). We are given a very full picture of the family, but one item of information comes as a complete surprise: the father, Thomas, is dead! Obviously there was an error in that 1856 marriage certificate in not indicating that the groom's father was deceased – and the Thomas Brydon signing it must have been the groom's brother, shown in this Census return as an eleven-year-old schoolboy.

We are not too pleased with this omission – it has cost us a lot of time looking for the post-1855 death of a man we now know to have been dead in 1851.

We can tentatively fill in some birth dates, bearing in mind what I have already said about the reliability or otherwise of these stated ages. A typical example is William, here shown as 13 years old but appearing five years later on his marriage certificate as 21 years old.

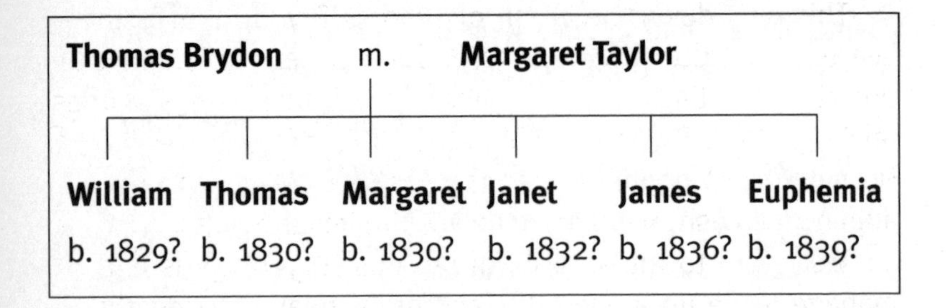

One little glimpse into life in Leith at this time is provided by the large number of entries for Redfords Close, where a woman's occupation column carries the note 'has a mangle'. Clearly, in these pre-tumble-dryer days, capital investment in a mangle could show some return!

The civil registration and the census returns have pointed to one fact for the next stage of our search: the family seems to have been well established in the parish of South Leith and this is where we must look for information in the OPRs.

Again the procedure changes. We look up the master list of OPRs held in New Register House and see that there is a fairly complete collection of records for South Leith between 1800 and 1855. We take Euphemia as the youngest of the children shown in the 1851 Census returns and look for a possible birth entry around 1849. We request the volume containing birth records for South Leith for this year, indicating on our requisition slip that we want OPR 69212 (South Leith), the volume containing the year 1849.

This time we are in luck, finding a well-kept book, beautifully written and with the surnames clearly picked out in each page. We find an entry for Euphemia Brydon and find that she was born posthumously to Thomas Brydon and his wife Margaret Taylor.

This pins down the death of Thomas Brydon, but is the last piece of luck Pauline is to find in her search. The rest of our allocated time is spent trying to track down other entries relating to the Brydon family in the OPRs of South Leith. No mention in baptisms, banns or burials! We turn to the adjoining parish of North Leith – with similar results.

We return to the security of the post-1855 records and manage to tie up a few odds and ends, relating to deaths and offspring of people already identified in our chart, but no lead to extend our tree backwards.

The Census records prove particularly elusive. None of the people in our chart seem to figure in trade directories and the addresses given on Births, Marriages and Deaths near Census dates turn out not to apply when we come to look at the Census returns. A long, long search – with little to show for it after the early successes. We certainly have a few long shots which we can pursue later, but in general Pauline's search has had disappointing results.

CASE HISTORY TWO

Bob Leitch produces a case history which is in many instances the exact opposite of Pauline's. Whereas she started precisely and finished up with a misleading error in the records and complete lack of success in the OPRs, Bob starts with a considerable stutter and finishes up with a jackpot – an 1855 death – followed up by a fine run in the OPRs.

The initial stutter comes about because Bob sets off with the wrong Christian name for his grandfather – a not uncommon failure in instances where someone is recalling a grandparent who died when one was young! After some fruitless delving in the indexes, Bob phones his mother and comes back with the correct Christian name, and from that moment he never looks back – if that's the right phrase.

Bob starts off then with only a name and an approximate date, giving him a starting point something like this:

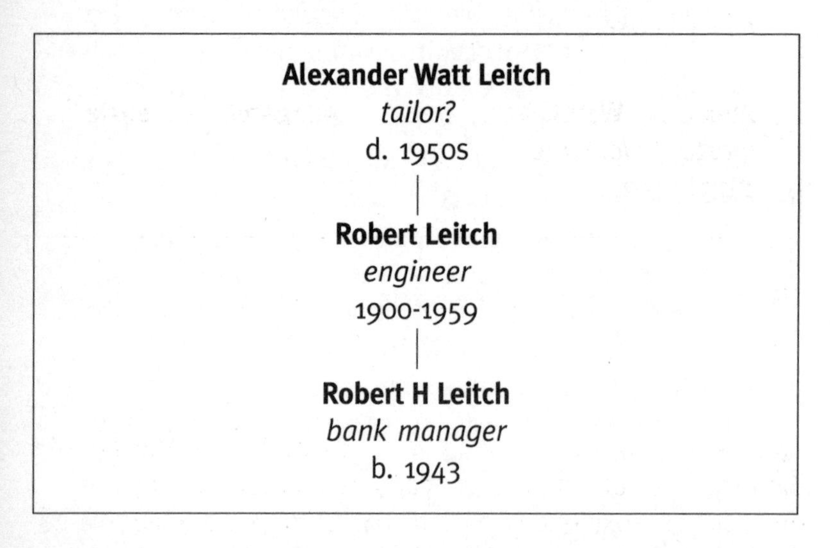

We have the advantage of a not-too-common surname, Leitch – and a fine and distinctive combination of Christian names, Alexander Watt – to help us get off to a good start. We look through the indexes for Male Deaths around the early 1950s and find for 1952 a death entry for Alexander Watt Leitch for St Andrews, Edinburgh, 296. We go through the routine – and are soon copying down the details on the headed pages of our notebook. In amongst the usual facts we find that Bob's grandfather was a master tailor/cutter, that he died at the age of 77 at Leslie Place in Edinburgh and, key facts for our investigation, his parents were master-baker Robert Leitch and Hepburn Woodcock. (We note in passing that he was married to Margaret MacKenzie, a fact to be stored away on his personal sheet as the subject of a later search perhaps.)

Robert Leitch *master baker*	m.	**Hepburn Woodcock**
Alexander Watt Leitch *master tailor/cutter* 1875?-1952	m.	**Margaret MacKenzie**

We are in luck. You don't get many names as distinctive as Hepburn Woodcock – and hers is obviously the name we can pick for our index searching.

That combination of names is so distinctive that we can bypass looking for Alexander Watt Leitch's birth certificate to find the date of his parents' marriage and look backwards from his approximate birth date (1874) for a marriage. We go back quite a way (to 1860) before coming across a Hepburn Woodcock in the Female Marriages. Even with such an unusual name, we still check that there is an equivalent partner (Robert Leitch) in the 1860 Male Marriages to show that this really is *our* pair.

Through the routine – and we are looking at the actual entry once again. Robert Leitch, a baker, aged 22, lived at 14 Bedford Street, Edinburgh, the son of Adam Leitch, a fishmonger, and Isabella Orr. He married Hepburn Woodcock of 3 Leggats Land, Stockbridge, 22-year-old daughter of William Woodcock, an upholsterer, and Hepburn Anderson.

This enables Bob to add a couple of blocks to the next generation band.

Adam Leitch *fishmonger* m. **Isabella Orr**		**William Woodcock** *upholsterer* m. **Hepburn Anderson**
|		|
Robert Leitch b. 1838? married 1860, Edinburgh	m.	**Hepburn Woodcock** b. 1838?

From the age of the groom, we deduce that he, Robert Leitch, was born around 1838. His parents' marriage would not therefore appear in the post-1855 records. Neither of them, however, is shown to be dead at the time of his marriage in 1860, so it is worth trying, despite our chastening experiences of a similar situation in the case of Pauline, to find the death of the father, Adam Leitch. The name is unusual enough to avoid too many false alarms – and the family seems to be localised in Edinburgh. We work forward on Male Deaths from 1860 and it takes us a long and hefty spell at the large volumes before we find in the index for 1888 an entry for the death of an Adam Leitch.

By this time, the indexes are showing the age of deceased people. This man is shown as 73 years old – so we are in the right area. We go for the original entry.

A quick check at the occupation, and it seems certain he is ours – his occupation is given as 'fishmonger' and his wife, deceased, is Isabella Orr.

Key facts among those entered on our notepad are that his parents were Robert Leitch, butler, and Catherine Anderson.

So Bob can now tag on Adam Leitch's parents and go back another generation.

Robert Leitch m. **Catherine Anderson**
butler

Adam Leitch m. **Isabella Orr**
fishmonger d. before 1888
1815?-1888

This is where we have an unexpected turn of luck. Before going on to either the Census returns or the OPRs, we decide to see if we can find a Robert Leitch, that butler (top left) dying after 1855. We look at the 1855 returns and there, sure enough, in Edinburgh is a Robert Leitch! This is the great jackpot year – can it possibly be our Robert Leitch, the father of Adam Leitch (1815-1888)?

We chance our arm and ask to see the entry. It is a Robert Leitch of the right age. And he was married to a Catherine Anderson – he must be our man. But he is not a butler – his occupation is given as labourer! And in this great year of 1855, we have the added bonus of a list of all his children, living and dead! We look through them for a sign of our Adam Leitch. Among the seven children, no son called Adam. Disappointment – until we notice that the informant is . . . Adam Leitch, fishmonger and son of the deceased.

A son who had left his own name off the list of children! We have found our man – beyond a shadow of a doubt – and learnt the lesson of peering at every column for the smallest scrap of information.

Bob's bullseye of an 1855 birth certificate is a very valuable one indeed. Here is some of the wealth of data carried by that single entry:

1. Robert Leitch died on 27 September 1855. The place was given as the Water of Leith – not, in fact, a drowning in the water that runs through Edinburgh but the name given then to the delightful village now known as Dean Village.
2. He had died of paralysis which he had had for eight years (this often refers to the effects of a stroke).
3. He had been married to Katherine Anderson, slightly different spelling of the Christian name but confirmation of the information given on their son's (Adam's) death certificate. Katherine was still alive at the time of Robert's death.
4. Robert was 74 years old and had lived at his present address for 50 years.
5. He had been born in Kirkcaldy in Fife.
6. He was buried in Dean Cemetery.
7. His father was John Leitch, coal miner, and his mother Sophia Penman.
8. He and Katherine had had the following children (as at 1855), Robert (dead), Helen (47 years old), Mary (43), Andrew (42), James (dead), Jessie (dead), Thomas (dead) and of course Adam, confirmed by the informant's details but left out of the list.

Just look what this adds to the family tree:

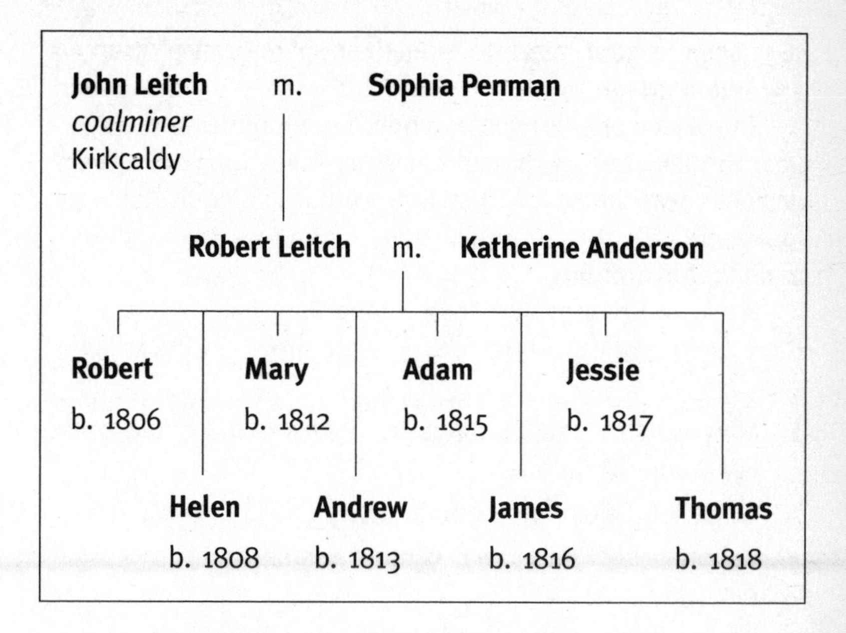

That information provides a suitable climax to the searches among the post-1855 records, allowing us to add a lot of detail to the Robert Leitch corner of our tree.

At this stage we have two main alternatives open to us:

1 Go on to the OPRs and try and extend the tree backwards.

2 Consolidate and expand the information on the existing people through Census returns and other post-1855 records.

We opt for the Census returns to start off with and go up to the library.

THE CENSUS RETURNS

With Robert and his family clearly settled in the Water of Leith for some time, the Census returns for that village for

1851 seem a good place to start to see if we can pick up any information.

The Water of Leith comes under Edinburgh so we are able to make use of the street/district index for 1851 to help narrow down the search. Usual procedures – requisition slip indicating CEN 1851 and the books – bring us the enumerator's returns.

Book 25 Entry 37 (we took a long time finding that as there were no house numbers or even streets in the village) shows:

1 Mary Leitch, head, W, aged 32, provision merchant, born Edinburgh St Cuthberts.
2 Catherine Leitch, mother, 64, also b. St Cuthberts.
3 Robert Leitch, father, 63, gentleman's servant, b. Kirkcaldy.
4 Jamima Healy, daughter, 6, scholar, b. St Cuthberts.

This provides us with a fine cameo of the family group. Robert and Catherine are living with their daughter, Mary, and 6-year-old granddaughter, Jamima. But Mary is a widow (the letter W), although she is entered under her maiden name of Leitch and not her married name of Healy, and the fact that she is down as a provision merchant suggests that she is carrying on her husband's business. Water of Leith, as we see from the other returns on the Census, was very much a centre for flour and meal milling alongside the fast-flowing stream and close to the big population centre of Edinburgh.

There is no doubt that this is our Robert, but once again we have the gentleman's servant description. Water of Leith was very handy indeed for the big houses of the New Town's West End, which could support our first record of him but does not correspond with his death certificate information.

We also see for our later investigations that the rest of the family were all born in the St Cuthberts parish – a fact that will simplify our searches.

We incidentally take a look at the 1841 Census details for the Water of Leith just to see if there is anything of value – this Census was bare in the extreme and not usually worth pursuing if you have enough details from elsewhere. Robert is shown as a labourer this time – and they seem to have got his wife and daughter mixed up as far as ages and names are concerned (the Census does not include relationships).

Going back to the marriage of his grandson Robert Leitch and Hepburn Woodcock in 1860, we see another opportunity for expanding the family lines as the marriage comes close to the 1861 Census.

We go through the same routine and look for Census returns for the two addresses shown for the bride and groom.

14 Bedford Street, Edinburgh 68511 Entry 25.

We are in luck again, for here we find, a year after the marriage, the groom's family still living at the address – and a large family it is, thanks to the fact that Robert was one of the older offspring and a number of his younger sisters were still living with their parents:

1 Adam Leitch, head, 46, fishmonger.

2 Isabella Leitch, wife, 46.

3 Mary, daughter, unmarried, 18, dressmaker.

4 Jean, daughter, unmarried, 15, dressmaker.

5 Helen, daughter, 9, scholar.

6 Henrietta, daughter, 7, scholar.

7 Catherine, daughter, 3.

8 Mary McRoberts, boarder, 19, servant.

All except the servant are shown as born in Edinburgh.

Among the other families occupying the building are a cabinetmaker, a woodcarver, a housepainter, a jeweller and a bootmaker.

This allows us to extend the family tree sideways and to pencil in a few tentative birth dates:

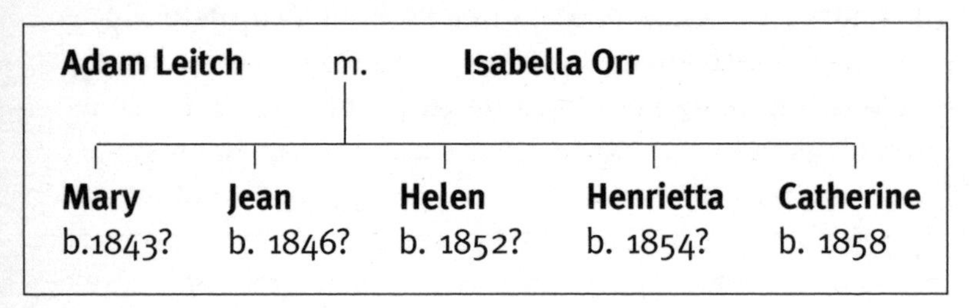

When we come to look at the bride's address from that 1860 marriage, we have a little initial difficulty, resulting from the fact that there seems to be no entry for 3 Leggats Land – but do find the family living at 1 Haugh Street, which may be the same place (closes and vennels often carried either their own name or the number of the street which marked their entrance). We may just have been lucky in having the family staying close by the bride's original home. The entry shows that the young couple were sharing their home with the wife's father:

1. Robert Leitch, head, aged 23, baker, born Edinburgh.
2. Hepburn Leitch, wife, 23, born Dundee.
3. Hepburn Leitch, daughter, one month, b. Edinburgh.
4. William Woodcock, lodger, widower, 52, upholsterer, b. Dundee.
5. Jamima Woodcock, lodger, 17, b. Edinburgh.

This again gives a nice rounded profile of the family: the

young couple with new baby, dutifully and traditionally named after the maternal grandmother (and incidentally in this case, the mother), providing a home for the widowed grandfather, William, and for the wife's sister, Jamima.

The fact that Hepburn was born in Dundee and her sister Jamima in Edinburgh suggests that the family started in Dundee but between 1838 (birth of older sister) and 1842 (birth of younger sister) moved to Edinburgh. All are items to be noted down for future reference.

The family, incidentally, seem well housed at 1 Haugh Street, having three rooms which possess one or more windows.

THE POST-1855 REGISTRATIONS

The original work plus the Census returns have given us a large number of people to track down in greater detail in the Births, Marriages and Deaths records. We therefore have a spell down with the indexes again to try and pinpoint some of the events. Among the records we find the following:

Births

1. Hepburn Leitch, the little baby mentioned in the 1861 Census returns – and her subsequent brothers, William, Adam, James and Alexander Watt Leitch (the man we started with).
2. Catherine Leitch, the three-year-old daughter of Adam Leitch shown in the 1861 Census returns for 14 Bedford Street.

Deaths

We find the death of Isabella Orr, wife of Adam Leitch (1883) and William Woodcock, father of Hepburn Woodcock (1878).

This gives us a pair of parents in each case, allowing us to extend Isabella Orr's line thus:

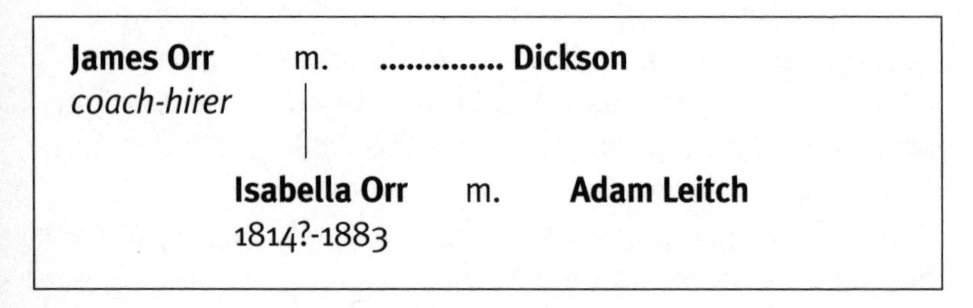

Notice that the person reporting Isabella's death (her husband Adam) did not know the Christian name of his mother-in-law, although he did know her maiden surname.

William Woodcock, the Dundee upholsterer, has his line extended as follows:

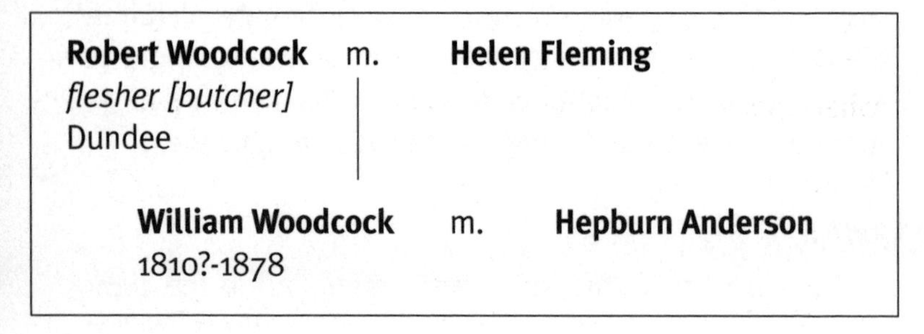

A surprising death we found was that of Bob Leitch, whom we had identified as the father of Alexander Watt Leitch and the groom in the 1860 marriage to Hepburn Woodcock. He died at the very early age of 39, the victim of apoplexy, leaving his wife to cope with four children.

BACK TO THE OPRS

With so much information collected from civil registration and census returns we are well equipped to tackle the daunting field of the Old Parochial Records.

The first target is the background for Robert Leitch, the butler/labourer who moved to Water of Leith after 1800, but who had been born in Kirkcaldy around 1780, the son of John Leitch, coal miner, and Sophia Penman. The two unusual names give us some hope, and we plunge into the OPRs for Kirkcaldy, requisitioning the volume carrying birth entries for that period.

We come up with a good round nothing. Well, almost nothing. We find the odd Leitch (now spelt Leech) and Penman (and even a Sophia or two), but none that tie in firmly with our jigsaw pieces. We try the marriage records, looking for a Leitch marrying a Penman – and find a Penman marrying a Leitch. We find marriage records of a number of what appear to be Robert's brothers – all sons of John Leech, coal-grieve at Smitton, but no definite sign of our man. We look at the meagre death records – and come across the death of a John Leech, son of Andrew Leech, coal-hewer, and a victim of the smallpox epidemic which swept the little community in 1773, but, with no clue as to his age even, we cannot assume it is the John Leech we are looking for.

Reluctantly, amid all the echoes of the family we are seeking, we call it a day.

Our searches in the OPRs in what is left of our nominal week of searching are confined to the branches other than the main Leitch line. (Even in these days of sex equality, it is the custom to consider the male, name-bearing line as the main one, although genealogy is a hobby in which anything goes, and the person who seeks to find as much as possible about all the families that went into producing him has a load of work on his hands but is adopting a perfectly legitimate stance.)

The children of Adam Leitch and Isabella Orr

These children are already clearly listed in our Census returns but we are able, through the St Cuthberts Edinburgh parish records, which are well kept and (glory be!) well indexed in typescript books, to get details of the birth of every one and keep track of the numerous house moves of Adam and Isabella. We trace a few that were not included in the Census returns and find that Henrietta was in fact baptised Heneratia, clearly in memory of an uncle – a long run of girls had perhaps led the parents to give up hope of ever producing a male to bear the name!

The forebears of Katherine Anderson

Having failed with the line of Robert Leitch, 1780?-1855, we try his wife Katherine Anderson, knowing that she had been born in St Cuthberts (census detail). We find her baptismal entry for 1780 and the record of her parents' marriage on 6 July 1760, giving us the names of two of Bob's great-great-great-great-great-grandparents – George Anderson, a miller in the Water of Leith, and William Law, a shoemaker in the same village.

The forebears of Isabella Orr

Similarly, we are in luck with the forebears of Isabella Orr, who married Adam Leitch on 24 March 1837. We are able to find in the well-documented St Cuthberts parish records her baptismal entry for December 1814, and the marriage record of her parents on 17 July 1798 which gives us the full name of her mother Isabella Dickson. You will remember that her death certificate was lacking on this point. For the first time, the family tree protrudes outside Scotland: Isabella Dickson's father was a baker in Liverpool.

The result of all that searching is to provide Bob with an impressive family tree which looks something like the chart overleaf. And that is surely a very substantial platform on which to base any future research into the family history.

Of course, we have only followed the line from one of Bob's grandparents – Alexander Watt Leitch. He has three others to pursue if he's really hooked on the New Register House records!

This is of course not the end of the story. Bob can use what he has discovered to lead on to areas of exploration in other archives, to books to read on the Water of Leith, to museums to visit to let him know something about life in Fife or the early years of Scottish coal mining.

JUST HOW GOOD IS THE IGI?

Thinking that I might have overpraised the conjuring powers of the LDS FamilySearch site in tapping in to the IGI, I carried out a simple experiment.

I took Bob Leitch's family tree, the one we had managed to build up in our token week and which had posed a couple of dead ends, and set about trying to extend it from my PC at home, using only the IGI files.

The results were astonishing.

At the top left of the tree we had John Leitch, coal miner, married to Sophia Penman. Using FamilySearch, I found:

1 A date for the marriage.

2 Date of Sophia Penman's birth.

3 Names of her parents.

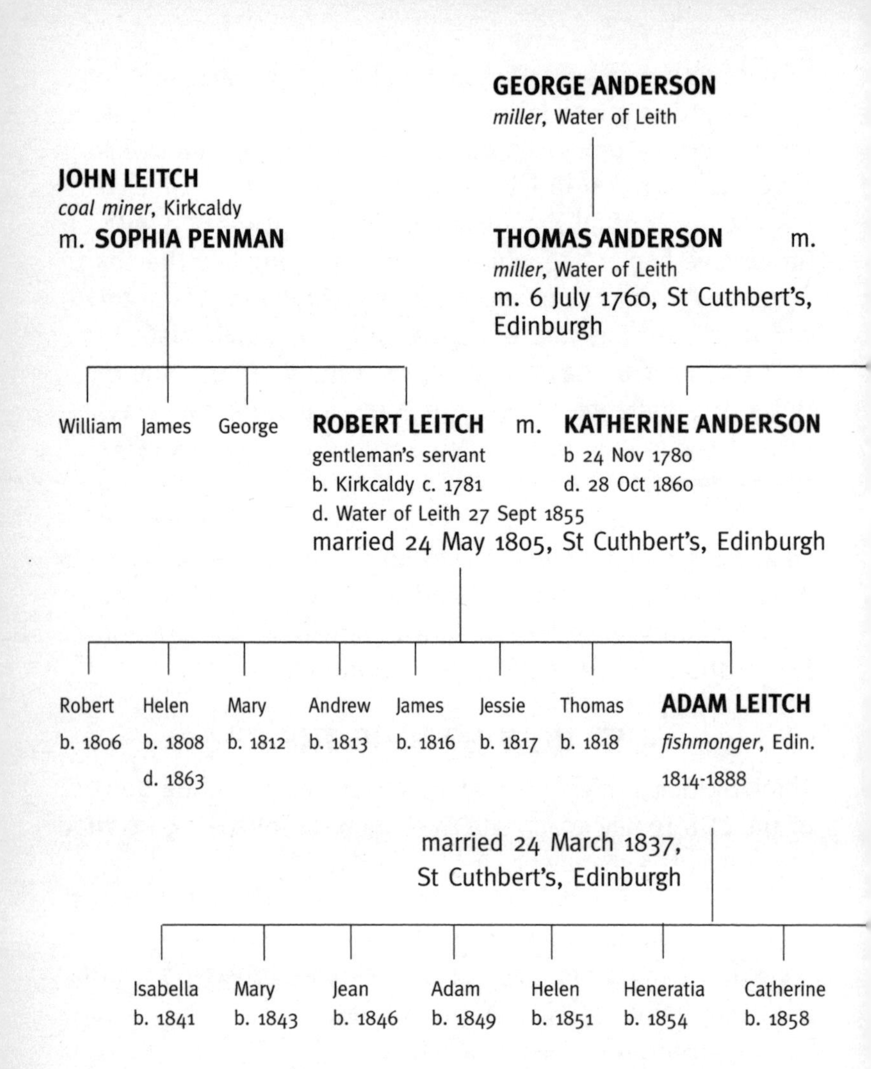
GEORGE ANDERSON
miller, Water of Leith
JOHN LEITCH
coal miner, Kirkcaldy
m. SOPHIA PENMAN
THOMAS ANDERSON
m.
miller, Water of Leith
m. 6 July 1760, St Cuthbert's, Edinburgh
William
James
George
ROBERT LEITCH
gentleman's servant
b. Kirkcaldy c. 1781
d. Water of Leith 27 Sept 1855
m.
KATHERINE ANDERSON
b 24 Nov 1780
d. 28 Oct 1860
married 24 May 1805, St Cuthbert's, Edinburgh
Robert
b. 1806
Helen
b. 1808
d. 1863
Mary
b. 1812
Andrew
b. 1813
James
b. 1816
Jessie
b. 1817
Thomas
b. 1818
ADAM LEITCH
fishmonger, Edin.
1814-1888
married 24 March 1837,
St Cuthbert's, Edinburgh
Isabella
b. 1841
Mary
b. 1843
Jean
b. 1846
Adam
b. 1849
Helen
b. 1851
Heneratia
b. 1854
Catherine
b. 1858

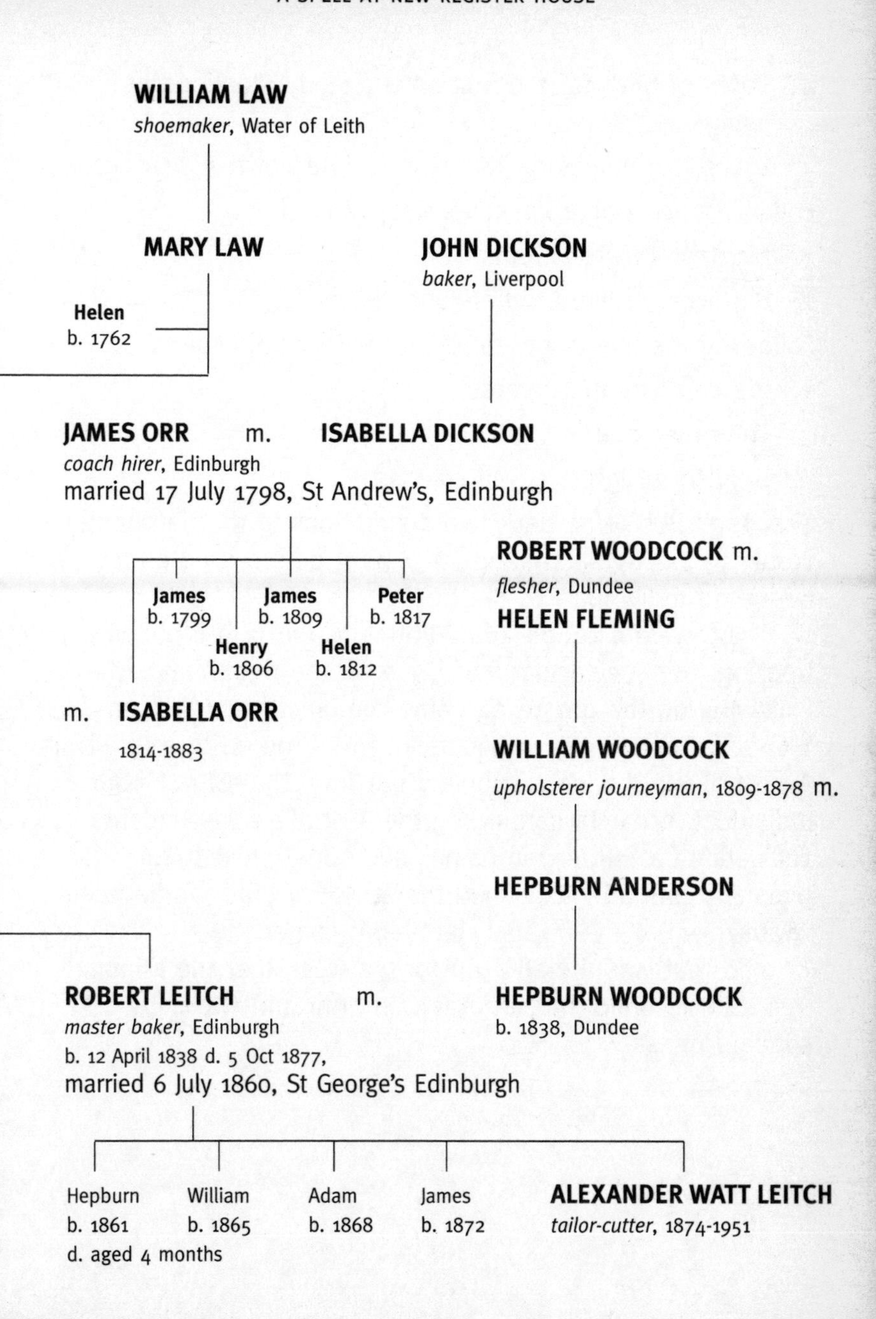
WILLIAM LAW
shoemaker, Water of Leith
MARY LAW
JOHN DICKSON
baker, Liverpool
Helen
b. 1762
JAMES ORR
m.
ISABELLA DICKSON
coach hirer, Edinburgh
married 17 July 1798, St Andrew's, Edinburgh
ROBERT WOODCOCK m.
flesher, Dundee
HELEN FLEMING
James
b. 1799
James
b. 1809
Peter
b. 1817
Henry
b. 1806
Helen
b. 1812
m.
ISABELLA ORR
1814-1883
WILLIAM WOODCOCK
upholsterer journeyman, 1809-1878 m.
HEPBURN ANDERSON
ROBERT LEITCH
m.
HEPBURN WOODCOCK
master baker, Edinburgh
b. 12 April 1838 d. 5 Oct 1877,
married 6 July 1860, St George's Edinburgh
b. 1838, Dundee
Hepburn
b. 1861
d. aged 4 months
William
b. 1865
Adam
b. 1868
James
b. 1872
ALEXANDER WATT LEITCH
tailor-cutter, 1874-1951

4 Dates of birth for the four sons already identified by name.
5 Dates and names of five more children of the marriage.

Following up Sophia Penman's line, I found:

1 Marriage of her parents.
2 Baptisms of five brothers and sisters.

Following the line of her father, John Penman, I found:

1 His baptism and parents.
2 Their marriage in 1708.
3 Baptism of John's seven siblings.

That took Bob's line back two generations in that left-hand corner to a six-greats grandfather born before 1700 and added 22 individuals to the tree!

There were a couple of additions to the centre of Bob's tree, but the spectacular find came on the right-hand side. Following up the promising name combination of William Woodcock and Hepburn Anderson, I was routed to a Family Ancestral File (i.e. data supplied not from the IGI but from individual research) chronicling the Australian descendants. That added a further ten names and some present-day relatives and probably explained the arrival of that middle name 'Watt' down at the bottom right-hand corner.

And that was a matter not of the week that the original tree took to build, but less than an hour and two cups of coffee. Honest!

EIGHT

The National Archives of Scotland

A tantalising treasure dome of the nation's documentary heritage. If your ancestors are there, how can you track them down?

> 'Lauritz La Cour and James Boyd should accept of my curious collection of walking sticks one each for their own use, but I wish them to give one each to those of my intimate friends as they may think would prize them.'

This sentence comes at the end of a long and rather dreary will made by a Leith businessman and couched in the flat language of his lawyer. Only when he comes to add a sentence to express his thanks in advance to his two friends and executors does his own language show through and we get this delightful glimpse of a character as opposed to a combination of a name, a profession and the dates which bracket a life.

The passage sets the tone for the sort of information which we are likely to find at the second great base for our ancestor-hunting – Register House, another elegant Georgian edifice, more prominently sited than GRO, and the home of the National Archives of Scotland, the archives formerly known as SRO (Scottish Record Office).

Here the amount of material is enormous, the bulk eclipsing even the store of New Register House and spilling over from the East end of Princes Street to the West end, to the repository, West Register House, at Charlotte Square. To confuse the visitor, the latter is not in West Register Street, which in fact runs alongside New Register House.

Not only is the bulk of the material so great, its nature is much more unmanageable than those records of Births, Marriages and Deaths that we have been studying.

It is essential that we have a very clear picture at this stage of just who our ancestors were, what they did and where they lived. The work we have done at GRO so far will help us make the most of what NAS has to offer.

Once again, the first step is to 'sign on' – and in this case it is not going to cost you anything. All you are required to do is make your way to the Historical Search Room and let them know what it is you are after. Family research, the family name and the area should be enough. That information will enable the staff to get some idea of the sort of material you will want to look at – and allow them to give you the right sort of help. You will get a Reader's ticket, valid until the last day of the calendar year – and you should try and have this with you each time you visit Register House.

The material is, I must repeat, vast in scope and haphazard in nature. As you would expect from what I have already said, NAS has a website. Just look at the lists of topics they invite you to delve into – and they let you download useful fact sheets: Adoption, Buildings, Crafts and Trades, Crime and Criminals, Customs and Excise, Deeds, Divorce, Education, Emigration, Estate Records, Inheriting Lands and Buildings, Lighthouses, Military Records, The Poor, Sasines, Taxation Records, Valuation Rolls, Wills and Testaments.

We are clearly in a different world from the more precise boundaries of the GRO. Now more than ever it is vital to have precise background information if you are to stand any chance of striking gold.

You can add to your knowledge by reading Cecil J Sinclair's

Tracing Scottish Local History in the Scottish Record Office. It's a cracker of book, an object lesson in how to cover a large amount of complex material lucidly, comprehensively and with flair. You'll get it at good bookshops, the Stationery Office (formerly HMSO) and, of course, your nearest library.

I can't hope to scratch the surface of the book's (and the NAS's) treasures, but here, as a carrot to your endeavours, are some of the areas in which you may well be searching.

THE KIRK SESSION RECORDS

I'll start with one of the areas not covered in that website list – the Kirk Session Records. These recount the week-by-week business of the individual congregations in the Church of Scotland.

You may feel that this is an unpromising target for your efforts, but these were no mere reports of collection monies, purchase of hymn books or discussions on flower arrangements. The elders saw themselves very much as the guardians of every aspect of the community's life and this is reflected in the subjects covered.

Many of the NAS holdings have been produced in book form and the page overleaf comes from the Session Book of Rothesay. On that one page, there are some fifty individuals mentioned by name (a high proportion of what must have been a fairly small community), some with very colourful asides. If you can find the kirk session records for the parish in which your forebears lived you may very well find them mentioned in the pages, either as the elders dispensing moral judgements, or as parishioners at the receiving end of charity (in our extract you will see that Isobel N'Curdy received 'one pound two shillings four pennies for new cloaths – her old ones having been

THE SESSION BOOK OF ROTHESAY – 1635-1750

Hector's) spouse has compeired before the congregation three severall times but was not yet absolved and he had caused advertise her to attend this diet. And being called she compeired and her sin with its aggravations being set home on her conscience and she seeming serious and penitent was removed. The Session being satisfied with her appointed she might compeir once more before the congregation and be absolved, and she being called in the same was intimate to her.

Alexander Gray and Janet Spence have satisfied discipline and are absolved.

Session clos'd with prayer.

SESSION HELD AT ROTHESAY JUNE 19TH 1720

After prayer

Sederunt: Master Dugald Stewart, minister; James Stewart, provost, Thomas Wallace, bailiff; Robert Wallace, late bailiff; James, Edward and John Stewarts; Alexander and Donald Leeches; Robert Glass and John M'Conachy, elders; and John Gealy, Donald Nivin, Donald Bannatyne and William M'Gilcherran, deacons.

The severall ordinary collections since last accompt with the treasurer, November 4th, 1719, amount to 60 lib., 2s. 4d. which with 11s. 4d. that remained in his hands comes to 16 lib. 13s. whereof given to severall indigent persons and approven by the Session 15l. 12s. There remains 45l. 1s. 8d. whereof the Session appoints to be distribute in manner following, vizt. one pound four shillings Scots each to Helen Stewart, John Morison, Margaret Glass, Jeals N'Thomas, Janet Spence, Margaret Stewart, and Cathrine N'Arthur; and one lib. each to John M'Kinlay's orphans, Janet Gealy, Elspeth Black, Donald M'Neil, Gilbert M'Kinlay, Bryce Frazer, Elspeth Wallace, and Ninian Stewart; and sixteen shillings Scots each to Blind John M'Gilcherran, Walter M'Alaster, Catherine N'Conachy, Cathrine N'Alastar, Janet Beith, Isobel N'Curdy, Jane N'Gilcherran, and Isobel N'Neil; and thirteen shillings four pennies each to Mary N'Gillchattan, Donald M'Eachan, Mary Stewart, Mary Heman, James M'Tyre, Christian Nivin, Janet M'Gilcherran, Elspeth Frazer and Christian Campbell; *item* half a crown to help the payment of one Seymore's cure and one pound two shillings four pennies for new cloaths for Isobel N'Curdy (her old ones having been stollen), in all now distribute 31l. 8s. 4d., which taken from the abovesaid 45l. 1s. 8d, the treasurer remains debitor to the Session in 13l. 13s. 4d.

stollen'), or punishment (the pages are packed with moral pronouncements on backsliding among the faithful, generally as regards sexual relations!).

Sometimes the stories continue like some kind of eighteenth-century soap opera. In one Borders kirk, the parents of a newborn child were interrogated, not because they were unmarried, but because the birth had come a mere seven months after the marriage. The couple pleaded that the baby was born premature, but at the following session meeting the attending midwife was called and she declared that she'd been in the business for forty years and she could tell a full-term baby when she saw one. The harrassed mother failed to turn up at the next meeting, but at the following session, her father was hauled before the elders to explain why he had allowed the couple and their baby to abscond to Edinburgh rather than face further interrogation.

TESTAMENTS AND INVENTORIES

'You can't take it with you, but you can decide where it goes' is the basic principle behind wills and testaments – and the importance of making clear just what a dead man's wishes were has handed the legal profession one of its oldest and most cherished tasks: the recording of those wishes.

In Scotland, this act is restricted to the passing on of moveable property (land and buildings come into a different category, as we shall see later), but the documentation relating to it can cover a wealth of information about people and property, family history and financial states. The great accumulation of testaments (including wills where these were made, or testaments dative where the person did not leave express instructions) is for the most part housed in the Scottish Record Office, indexed (glory be!) and available, for the most part, in good condition and presented in very passable handwriting.

While the basic principle remains the same over the centuries – and indeed much of the language and glimpses into human nature are surprisingly similar – it is worth knowing that there were two main stages as far as the records are concerned. Up until 1822, all testaments were confirmed by the Commissary Courts of Scotland. The origin of these courts lay within the Church and this is reflected in the areas they cover, approximating roughly to the pre-Reformation dioceses Aberdeen, Argyll, Brechin, Caithness, Dunblane, Dumfries, Dunkeld, Edinburgh, Glasgow, Hamilton & Campsie, Inverness, The Isles, Kirkcudbright, Lanark, Lauder, Moray, Orkney & Shetland, Peebles, Ross, St Andrews, Stirling and Wigtown. These covered the testaments relating to their own area, except for Edinburgh which also exercised an additional overall role, taking in testaments from the length and breadth of Scotland as well as those made by Scots outside their native land.

Fortunately, all testaments are indexed (in volumes according to the relevant Commissary Court), from the earliest recorded examples (ranging from 1514 in Edinburgh to 1700 in Wigtown) up to the year 1800. This work has been done by the Scottish Record Society (and it is unlikely that any of you will get very far in this genealogy game without giving thanks to that fine body!) and gives the Scot and his descendants a distinct advantage over his Sassenach neighbours in this respect.

From 1823 onwards, the Sheriff Courts took over responsibility for confirmation of testaments – and from that date until 1876 there is a little problem in that not all of the sheriff court confirmations are lodged in the Scottish Record Office – some have been kept by the sheriff clerks. From 1876 onwards, an annual list of testaments is issued and that provides a simple means of tracking down the testament you are looking for

So you want to see if there are any testaments to help you? (They will often be accompanied by inventories of just what was in the house when the person died, usually listed in staggering detail.) This is where your foundation work at GRO begins to pay off. You have the name of a person, the date of his death and the place where he died (although it may be that he made his will elsewhere, so it would be handy to know whether or not he spent his earlier life in some other part of Scotland). These details will give you some idea of just where you should begin your search. Before 1800, as you have seen, the printed indexes make the task more simple. After that date, you may need a little help from the staff in the first instance although you will soon get the hang of it. The filling in of requisition slips here is, thanks to the great variety of material held, much more complex than the procedure at GRO.

The information varies considerably with the complexity of the property being willed and the number of bequests and beneficiaries. You can find a wealth of genealogical information or very little, an abundance of personal detail or none at all, a sheaf of insights into the personality of the deceased or no inkling whatsoever. The uncertainty is part of the attraction.

COURTS OF LAW

Court cases are particularly fine sources of insight into the lives of Scots, high and low, so persevere with the rather haphazard wealth of indexes here. If you have an unusual name to investigate, just chance your arm and browse the indexes.

You may have received a tip-off from some earlier research. When I noticed that a particular tradesman's name disappeared from the directories to be replaced by his wife only to reappear a few years later, I suspected a bankruptcy. With a year and a name, I was able to track down the legal documents and unearth a wealth of family information. In the Condescension – a legal presentation to explain that the failure to pay a bill was not due to fraud or evil intent – some six pages of closely written text give a blow-by-blow account of the family involvement, lists other debts (including three tailors' bills to hint at a degree of extravagance) and even solved a genealogical mystery. The poor bankrupt explained that he took all the responsibilities on board because his brother had promised to help him out, 'but within months he had gone off to the East Indies'. So that's why I couldn't find brother Bob!

LAND OWNERSHIP AND SUCCESSION

The other great comprehensive funds of information are the *Registers of Sasines* (many and complex in the early years but gradually simplified until in 1926 they became a single central register). These relate to changes of land ownership while the *Services of Heirs* relate to succession and are well indexed after 1700, providing extracted information which may make it unnecessary to consult the original (often in Latin).

NINE

Time to Beachcomb the Web

The PC can deliver the world's biggest library to your home, augment the work you've already done and point the way ahead.

Those of you with a PC are now in a fine position to let yourself loose on the world wide web, in effect an enormous library where, from your desk or kitchen table or lap, you can surf, browse, or, in my own addition to the terminology, beachcomb to your heart's content.

The potential is infinite – which explains the proliferation of magazines devoted specifically to this side of genealogy. If you really get hooked, you'll have no difficulty tracking them down. I shall confine my remarks to offering what I believe to be the best starting point for anyone looking to understand more about their Scottish roots.

GENUKI describes itself as the UK and Ireland Genealogical Information Service and I've no quarrel with that. Just add in the Isle of Man and the Channel Islands just for good luck and you've got the full picture.

The website you're seeking is www.genuki.org.uk. That will take you into a compendium of information and other easily linked websites. In essence, it is built around a four-tier structure. In Scottish terms that works out like this:

- Top tier: the British Isles
- Tier two: Scotland
- Tier three: regions of Scotland
- Tier four: parishes in those regions

National

Steering through those levels is simple and at each level you will find a very similar array of topics. Go into Scotland and you'll find the information grouped under these headings: Archives and Libraries, Bibliography, Biography, Cemeteries, Census, Chronology, Church History, Church Records, Civil Registration, Correctional Institutions, Court Records, Description and Travel, Directories, Emigration and Immigration, Encyclopedias and Dictionaries, Gazetteers, Genealogy, Handwriting, Historical Geography, History, Land and Property Language and Languages, Law and Legislation, Maps, Merchant Marine, Migration, Internal, Military History, Names, Geographical, Names, Personal, Newspapers, Nobility, Occupations, Periodicals, Poorhouses, Poor Law, Population, Probate Records, Schools, Social Life and Customs, Societies, Statistics, and Taxation.

Click on any of them and see what you get.

Regional

Go down to the next layer, one of the counties/regions, and you will find the same sort of subjects on offer.

As an example of just what that all means, I explored Nairnshire on the south coast of the Moray Firth in the north-east of Scotland. Much of the information will be familiar, linking the county to the national records you will already have studied if that is the home of your forebears.

More localised information will give me a pen-picture of the area from a nineteenth-century publication and a map to make everything clearer.

It tells me that the area is served by the North East of Scotland Family History Society, with full details of its meetings and location, of its trailblazing research centre and of how the building work is progressing. It will lead me to the Society's website to list publications and let me order them. It will indicate research work in progress, including the logging of graveyard inscriptions.

The information at this tier level will vary considerably from one area to another, often according to the activity or otherwise of the local history society.

Parochial

At the next, the lowest tier – the parish – the information is even more unpredictable often with little at all to show. But the forest is newly planted and the landscape will not be recognisable in a year or two!

To show you what might be waiting for you, I looked at Hawick, one of the most heritage-conscious communities in the whole of Scotland. Many years ago, I addressed a large and receptive audience of the Hawick Archaeological Society, not on ancestry (I couldn't tell them anything about that back then) but on Scottish explorers.

The local worthy thanking me at the end of the evening explained why there were no Hawick men among my lengthy list of explorers: 'A day spent oot of Hawick is a day wasted!'

The audience and I appreciated what was, I am sure, a well-worn local *bon mot*.

Thanks to the long-running and intense track record of that Society, the Hawick pages are an Aladdin's Cave of goodies.

You'll find four of five dense pages giving you, for example, an 1806 description of Hawick, details of which gravestones have been logged, lists of books and articles about the town, including one on the local dialect, where to find a note of deaths of Hawick folk in Australia (so some did globetrot after all!) and dozens of links to other websites.

I repeat that this is one of the best examples. Don't expect to find such riches everywhere. But it may be, given the increasing tempo of activity in the family history societies, the sign of things to come.

Access to the world wide web will open up unpredictable avenues to explore. The range is almost incapable of definition. You must try it for yourself. But www.genuki.org.uk is the garden gate to these infinite delights. Open it.

TEN

The Libraries, Reference and Local

To the inexperienced, reference libraries can be offputting. Persevere – and the rewards could be enormous.

One person I was attempting to track down disappeared mysteriously from the Scottish records and re-appeared again many years later, with no hint as to how the intervening years had been spent. The clue came in a list of Edinburgh medical graduates which revealed that the thesis for which he had been awarded his MD was on the subject of the body structure of the alligator. With these creatures, to put it mildly, thin on the ground in the Highlands, this was, as it turned out, a pointer to missing years spent across the seas.

This little gem is typical of the kind of totally indefinable information which is carried in the reference libraries, the specialist libraries and the local libraries of Scotland, providing an insight sometimes into the genealogical details of a family but more often into the actual life of individuals.

Many people have been used to wandering along the fiction areas of libraries, with books grouped tidily by author, and all the Agatha Christies side by side, or along open reference shelves with all the goodies on display – the dictionaries of quotations, the atlases and the guides to butterflies of Great Britain. To such readers, the mysteries of the large reference libraries, where the shelves represent just the tip of the iceberg, may seem unfathomable.

Getting to grips with this type of reference library can pay very large dividends for the ancestor-hunter and it is worth the effort to achieve that familiarity. Two factors operate in favour of the newcomer:

Firstly, the librarians themselves. In these days of changing attitudes to service and the public, librarians along with postmen have mercifully retained the old-fashioned virtues of caring and cheerfulness. So if you can pick a time when they are not too busy, make yourself known to the librarians – explain your unfamiliarity with the system and spell out just what it is you are hoping to find, even if that gives away an understandable vagueness at this stage.

Secondly, there are the indexes, the heart of any reference library. Browse through them, get to know them. Note any fascinating section which you feel may be of interest.

What you are searching for will not be a straightforward item such as those we have been speaking about at GRO or even NAS. Now it will be very dependent on the facts which you have unearthed at those earlier stages. You may not even know that the information which relates to you exists, let alone where it is in the library. Serendipity, the art of making fortunate discoveries, is now a major partner in your efforts. But you must give it a chance to operate by exposing it to all the possible areas where luck can play a part.

It is difficult for me to tell anyone what to look for at this stage, but here are just a few random thoughts, with illustrations, to whet your appetite and keep you browsing at the reference shelves and indexes.

TRADE DIRECTORIES

Started for the larger urban centres in the second half of the eighteenth century, trade directories at first were concerned very much with the gentry and the professional men. Rapidly, they came to be service guides, very much the Georgian Yellow Pages of Scotland, where you could find a pastrycook or a cowfeeder, a surgeon or an artificial-leg maker.

Selections of these directories will be available at the big reference libraries and indeed at the libraries you have already been using at New Register House and Register House, but the really fine runs will be held in the relevant area library. For example, the Edinburgh Room at Edinburgh Central Library will be the place to go if you are looking for a continuous set of Edinburgh and Leith street directories, the Mitchell library if you are focused on Glasgow.

The information carried in these directories is enormous. They usually list people alphabetically, by street and by occupation. Bear in mind the following points:

1 The directories are trade publications – they may therefore throw more light on what your forebears did than did the civil registration. One of my wife's ancestors was described in some fourteen entries in the statutory registers (births, marriages and deaths of his children) as a copper engraver. Only in the street directories did we find that, although he was indeed a copper engraver, he was in fact a specialist engraver of sheet music. The later street directories even give a person's employer in many instances. An insurance clerk may have the information 'Sun Fire' added in brackets, a printer may have his publication added, a publican the name of his inn.
2 Trade directories may often give a person's trading address and his home address. This can provide a useful guide to, for example, the extent or growth of a person's business. I followed the progress of a pharmacist from one shop (1865 directory) to five shops (1876 directory) in this way.
3 Trade directories sometimes specify activities not mentioned in even the Census returns. In particular they list the jobs of women – where these are not specified in

either Census or registration returns. A person who was never more than a mother-and-wife statistic in the OPRs appeared as a sicknurse in the street directory. Another, recorded in the Census as hatmaker, appeared in the directory as a 'maker of fine Leghorn bonnets'.

4 Trade directories often go well beyond the boundaries of the city to take in small townships on the outskirts and country gentry. Check this.
5 Directories usually carried additional advertising – take a look at these announcements, especially if the person you are tracking was in the type of self-employed business that needed promotion.
6 Directories carried a great deal of additional information on the day-to-day lives of the citizens, rather as a good telephone directory does today. Take a look at these pages.

LISTS OF GRADUATES AND STUDENTS

Universities and schools have published useful directories which provide information that often goes much further than one would expect. I picked at random (promise!) two such directories, for Glasgow University and for Aberdeen Grammar School, and opened them at random (again, I promise!) to show the variety of information that is given and, I hoped, the potential gems which lurked in such columns.

The Glasgow University lists gave ample examples of the extremes that you are likely to encounter.

As you see, if you were unlucky enough to be searching for Robert Dickie (number 3 on the page) you would be disappointed to come away with only the information that he was Hibernus (Grad Albi and MD 1842) – guaranteed to send

ROLL OF GRADUATES **153**

DICKIE, MATTHEW **M.A. 1876**
Minister of South U.P. Church, Sanquhar

DICKIE, MATTTEW MURE **M.A. 1870, B.D. 1874**
Sometime U.P. Minister at Haddington; resigned in 1886, owing to ill-health; resided in Bristol, 1896.

DICKIE, ROBERT **M.D. 1842**
"Hibernus" [Grad. Alb.]

DICKIE, ROBERT **M.A. 1887**
Schoolmaster in (1) South Public School, Paisley, (2) Central Public School, Gourock, (3) Kibble Reformatory Insitution, Paisley, (4) Hutchesons' Grammar School, Glasgow, (5) Public School, Skelmorlie.

DICKIE, ROBERT PITTENDRIGH **M .A. 1885**
F.C. Minister at Longriggend.

DICKIE, WILLIAM **M.D. 1844, C.M. 1863**
Belize, Honduras

DICKIE, WILLIAM **M.A. 1875**
U.P. Minister at (1) Roseharty, (2) Perth, (3) Dowanhill, Glasgow

DICKINSON, JOHN **M.A.1883, B.Sc. 1886, M.B., C.M. 1887**
Campbeltown; Kirkdale, Liverpool; died at Kintillo, Bridge of Earn, 13th September 1890.

DICKINSON, ALEXANDER **LL.D. 1879**
M.O. Edinburgh 1860; Professor of Botany in (1) The School of Physic in Ireland 1866 to 1868, (2) Glasgow University, 1868 to 1879, (3) Edinburgh University, 1879 to 1887; born in Edinburgh, 21st February, 1836; died suddenly, of heart disease, on 30th December, 1887, during the interval of a curling match at Thriepland Pond, near Hartree, his residence in Peebleshire.

DICKSON, ALEXANDER **M.B., C.M. 1883**
Ship Surgeon; Baillieston; Yeovil, Somerset

DICKSON, CHARLES SCOTT **M.A. 1871**
(1) Writer, Glasgow; (2) Advocate, Edinburgh; Lecturer in Constitutional Law and History in Glasgow University during Summer, 1878; Solicitor-General for Scotland, 1876; Q.C. 1896; brother of James Douglas Hamilton Dickson, M.A. (q.v.).

DICKSON, DAVID **D.D. 1824**
Minister of (1) High Church, Kilmarnock, (2) St Cuthbert's, Edinburgh; died 28th July, 1842, aged 63; officiated at funeral of Sir Walter Scott.

DICKSON, GEORGE **M.D. 1824**
"Hibernus" [Grad. Alb.]

DICKSON, GEORGE **M.B., C.M. 1881, M.D. 1885**
Glasgow; son of Professor William Purdie Dickson (q.v.).

ABERDEEN GRAMMAR SCHOOL

DANIELSON, James Gordon **1896-1901**
[S. of Rev Andrew D., DD], Chindwara, India. b.15 February 1888. Entd. Lower I

In service of Bank of Scotland, 1904-1908; passed membership examination of the Institute of Bankers, Edinburgh, 1908; in service of Hongkong and Shanghai Banking Corporation in London, 1908-10; in Hamburg, 1910-11; in New York, 1911-15; in Yokohama, Japan, from December 1919.

2nd Lieut., Ist Highland Brigade, R.F.A. (T.F.), 6 Oct. 1915. Served in France and Belgium, with the 51st Highland Div., 1916; and with the Lahore Div., Sept. 1916-18. Acting Lieut., Nov. 1916; Lieut., Aug. 1917. Discharged 2 May 1919

DANSON, Arthur Llewelyn **1885-1889**
S. of Rev. J. M. D. 18 King Street. Age 10. Entd. Classical I

B.A. Oxon, 1898; passed into Indian Civil Service 1898; served in the Punjab as assistant commissioner; under-secretary to Government, 1905-7; registrar Chief Court, Punjab, 1908; died at Lahore as result of an accident, 27 March 1912.

DANSON, Edmund Wilmot **1887-1892**
S of Rev. J. Myers D., 18 King Street. Age 9. Entd. Middle I

Served an apprenticeship in Aberdeen White Star Line; attached to Royal Navy (Channel Squadron), 1897-8; joined Royal Indian Marine, 1899; engaged mostly on survey of coast of Persian Gulf and South India; took part in Somali Expedition (medal); died at Moulmein, Burma, as result of a shooting accident, 23 May 1921.

Naval Transport Officer, Bombay (lent from Royal Indian Marine). Commander, R.I.M. Jan. 1917

DANSON E(rnest) D(enny) Logie **1892-1894**
S. of Rev. [J. Myers} D, Ingleboro' House, Castlehill. Agd, 12 Entd. Classical I

M.A., 1902; tutor in York, 1902-4; student, Episcopal Theological College, Edinburgh, 1904-6; ordained deacon, 1906; priest 1907; assistant curate, S. Paul's Cathedral, Dundee, 1906-11; St Andrew's Cathedral, Singapore, 1911-12; acting chaplain in Java, 1913; chaplain of Seremban, F.M.S., 1914; bishop of Labuan and Sarawak, 1917. D.D. Aberd., 1921

Chaplain and Hon. Captain, Malay States Volunteer Rifles, 1 Jan. 1916. Resigned commission on appointment as Bishop of Labuan and Sarawak.

DANSON, James Gordon **1894-1903**
S. of Rev J. Myers D., Ingleboro' House, Castlehill, b. 1 March 1865. Entd. Middle I.

M.B., Ch. B., 1908; M.D. 1922; surgeon, Royal Navy, 1910

Served with Mediterranean Fleet, 1914; with Grand Fleet, 1915; in South Irish Waters (Queenstown) 1915; Egypt, 1916-17; at R.N. Barracks, Chatham, 1918. Surgeon Lieutenant-Commander 1918 (ante-dated to 1916).

DANSON, John Rhys **1897-1903**
S. of Rev. James [Myers] D., 19 Bon-Accord Crescent. B. 24 July 1887. Entd. Middle I.

Served apprenticeship as mechanical engineer with Messrs. Clyne, Mitchell & Company, Aberdeen; assistant engineer, Dundee Corporation Electricity Supply Department 1908; second engineer in the power station, La Plata, Buenos Aires, 1914; assistant municipal electrical engineer, Georgetown, Penang, S.S., 1919.

Private, 14th Batt. London regiment (London Scottish) (T.F.), 17 Dec. 1914. Served in France, June to Nov. 1916; in Salonika to June 1917; in Palestine to June 1918; in Belgium, to Feb. 1919. Sergt., 20 Dec. 1914; Company Sergt. Major, 4 June 1915; Regmtl Sergt. Major 22 Nov. 1916. Mentioned, 29 March and 25 Oct. 1917. D.C.M., 21 Aug. 1918. Demobd. 5 March 1919.

DAVIDSON, Alexander **1869-1870**
[S. of Alexander D.], Tarves. Age 17. Entd. II.

Farmer, Cairnhill and Little Meldrum, Tarves.

DAVIDSON, Alexander **1881-1886**
S. of Alexander D., Mains of Cairnbrogie, Tarves. Age 12. Entd. Middle II.

Entered service of Northern Assurance Company, Aberdeen, as junior clerk, 1889; now cashier.

DAVIDSON, Alexander **1884-1887**
S. of Rev. George D., Logie Coldstone, Dinnet. Age 14. Entd. Classical II.

Served apprenticeship with Messrs. Walker and Beattie, land surveyors, Aberdeen; in 1892, went to South Africa, subsequently becoming manager of the New Kleinfontein Gold Mining Company, Benoni; served as a volunteer throughout the South African War, receiving the Queen's Medal with four clasps; died at Kleinfontein Farm, Benoni, 9 January 1915.

DAVIDSON, Alexander Aitken **1900-[1907]**
S. of Thomas D., 13 Affleck Street. b. 3 April 1891. Entd. Lower II.

Of Messrs. Davidsons (Aberdeen), Limited, wholesale fish merchants, Aberdeen.

Private, 45th Battalion, Gordon Highlanders (T.F.), Oct 1914. Promoted Sergeant. 2nd Lieut.., 4th Batt. Gordon Highlanders, Nov. 1914. Served at home. Demobd. on medical grounds, 1917 (Lieut.)

DAVIDSON, Alexander Campbell **1904-1906**
S. of Alexander D., Bromhill Park. b 26 April 1896. Entd. Lower III

you scurrying to the introduction of the book to find just what that meant.

If, however, you were after Alexander Dickson (middle of the page) what a wealth of information is at your fingertips, including the information that he died suddenly of heart disease during the interval of a curling match at Thriepland Pond! I bet that wasn't all carried on his death certificate.

And if you were on the trail of David Dickson (three places down), what a real gem to come away with – he officiated at the funeral of Sir Walter Scott.

Obviously what went into those directories depended entirely on the information provided by the individuals. Indeed, penning this section, I felt so guilty that I for once filled in the form I get annually from my own college and let them know just what I had been doing over the years.

The Aberdeen Grammar School lists make much the same point. If you were looking for Alexander Davidson (second column, name two) you would gain little that would not arise from the Births, Marriages and Deaths. But if you were looking into the Danson family you would find five brothers on that same page. They seem moreover to provide the archetypal pattern for the great age of the international Scot – one a civil servant in the Punjab, one a bishop in Labuan, one a surgeon in the Royal Navy, one an engineer working from Buenos Aires to Penang, one a naval man and explorer.

Not for the first time, luck can play a big part in ancestor-hunting. But remember the words of one great golfer accused of being lucky: 'The more I practise, the luckier I get.'

Take a look at the other entries and get some feel of the potential of such a publication to anyone involved in not just tracing ancestors but learning something about their lives.

THE MINISTERS OF SCOTLAND

If you are very lucky, one of your ancestors will have been a minister in the Church of Scotland. Of all the professions, this is one which is arguably the best documented from the genealogist's point of view. The great *Fasti Ecclesiae Scotiae* details in many volumes the ministers ordained by the Church over the centuries. The entries seek to provide as much information as possible not only on the man's service within the Church but also on his family. Take a look at the page opposite, again selected at random. It relates to the south-west of Scotland (the early volumes are divided up according to the synod in which the minister worked) and refers to the parishes in Annan Synod of Hoddam, Ecclefechan and Luce.

Again, the amount of information varies mightily, but just ponder on some of those entries. Pick out the enormous amount of genealogical information – one could build up a fine family tree solely on the basis of that information. And consider the wealth of detail which would help solve what could be problem areas – it tells us that Alexander Orr's son John went off to be a merchant in Virginia, that Robert Menzies' son Lawrie drowned at Alexandrowsk, South Russia.

SESSION BOOKS

Keeping with the Church, it is worth mentioning that the Session Books kept at the NAS have in some areas been printed by local interests – and offer a much easier way of delving into the doings of your eighteenth-century ancestors. This is where the librarian will come in handy, knowing from your information which areas you are interested in. The local libraries are understandably the most likely source of this type of publication.

1681 WILLIAM CARNEGIE, M.A.; trans. from Careston in 1681; trans. to Arbroath after 3rd June 1686

1686 ALEXANDER GUTHRIE, M.A. (Edinburgh 1682); pres. by William, Duke of Queensberry, and Robert, Earl of Southesk, 24th and 27th May, coll. 26th Oct., and inst. 7th Dec, 1686; dep. by Presb. of Dumfries 16th June 1691, "for profaning the sacrament of baptism", etc. – [*G.R. Hornings, 7th July 1688; MS. Acc. of Min. 1689; Dumfries Presby. Reg.*]

1696 ANDREW DARLING, M.A.: ord. before 13th Oct 1696; trans. to Kinnoull between 11th May and 26th Dec. 1697,

1700 JAMES CURRIE, M.A. (Edinburgh 13 July 1695); licen. by Presb. of Earlston 16th Sept. 1697; called by Presb. *jure devoluto*, and ord. 9th May; 1700; died 25th Feb. 1726, aged 52. He marr. Isobel Bell, who survived him and had issue – James, min. of Middlebie; John; Andrew; Helen (marr. Thomas Bell in Westside of Blacksyke); Agnes; James; Sybella – (*Tombst*)

1729 ALEXANDER ORR, born 1686, son of Alexander O., min. of St Quivox; licen. by Presb. of Ayr 22nd June 1715; ord. to Muirkirk 5th June 1717; called 26 Feb., trans. and adm. 10th July, 1729; died 19th June 1767. He marr. 25 Jan 1722, Agnes (died 21st May 1760), daugh. of John Dalrymple of Waterside, and had issue – Agnes, born 9th Nov. 1722 (marr. William Young, min. of Hutton); Barbara, born 10th Oct..1723 (marr. John Craig, min. of Ruthwell); Alexander, W.S. born 23 March 1725, died 27th Nov. 1774; Peter, born 12th Oct. 1727; John, merchant, Virginia; Susan (marr. 1768, William Murray, second son of William M. of Murraythwaite) (*Tombst.*; M'Call's *Some Old Families.*)

1768 ALEXANDER BROWN, trans. from Tongland, and adm. 26th July 1768; trans. to Moffat 30th Oct 1783.

1784 JAMES YORSTOUN, born 17 Dec. 1755, son of Peter Y., min. of Closeburn; licen. by Presb. of Penpont 5th July 1775; ord. to Middlebie 23rd March 1778; pres. by William, Duke of Queensberry 8th Jan., and adm. 1st July 1784; died 6th April 1834. He marr., 2nd Oct. 1817, Margaret (died 25th March 1828), daugh. of James Currie Carlyle of Brydekirk. Publication – Account of the Parish (Sinclair's *Stat. Acc.* iii, xxi).

1834 ROBERT MENZIES, born 31st Jan 1801, son of William M., min. of Lanark; educated at the Grammar School there, High School, Edinburgh (dux 1816), and Univ. of Edinburgh; licen. by Presb. of Lanark, 4th August 1824; pres. by Lieut-General Matthew Sharpe of Hoddam, and ord. 2nd Sept. 1834; D.D. (Edinburgh, April 1864); died 6th July 1877. He marr. 28th Oct. 1835, Martha Reid (died 19 July 1875), daugh. of Robert Coldstream, merchant, Leith, and Elizabeth, daugh. of John Phillips, and had issue – William, min. of Duns; Robert Coldstream, born 11th July 1839, died 1st Sept. 1870; Allan, born 23 June 1841, died 29th Nov. 1892; John Coldstream, lieut., R.E., born 8th April 1843, died 2nd May 1866; Elizabeth Phillips, born 23rd June 1844, died 29 July 1865; Jeanie Newbigging, born 23rd Sept. 1845, died at Hyeres, France, 8th March 1892; Martha Reid Coldstream, born 12th April 1847, died 18th May 1914; Lawrie, engineer, born 16 June 1848, died at Alexandrowsk, South Russia, 11th Dec. 1914; Francis, born 22nd June, died 16th Dec. 1849; Alexander Charles, born 23 Aug. 1850, died 24th March 1875; Catherine Cowan, born 12th Oct. 1852, died 18th Oct. 1879. Publications – *Exposition of St Paul's Epistle to the Romans* (trans. from the German of F. A. Tholuck), 2 vols. (Edinburgh,1833-6); *Exposition, Doctrinal and Philological of Christ's Sermon on the Mount* (trans. from the German of F.A. Tholuck), 2 vols. (Edinburgh, 1834-7), *Answers to Robert Haldane's Strictures on Tholuck's Epistle to the Romans Edinburgh,* 1838); *Cuff, the Negro Boy*

SCOTLAND UNDER THE MINISTER'S EYE

Perhaps the finest work to come from a Church source was the massive *Statistical Account*, the brainchild of Sir John Sinclair, agriculturist, businessman and imaginative thinker. In the late 1700s, anxious to produce a definitive study of Scotland, he asked every parish minister in Scotland to produce a survey of his parish. Sinclair produced guidelines as to what they should look for – and the result of this enormous undertaking is to be found in most large reference libraries in Scotland. The success of Sinclair's venture can be judged by the fact that subsequent Statistical Accounts have been carried out from time to time, using a very similar basis for their scope and treatment.

By this stage, you will certainly have identified the parish in which your ancestors lived. You will also, if things have gone with even average smoothness, have got back to the sort of period (1790s) when this first *Statistical Account* was being prepared. You are now offered a thumbnail sketch (sometimes quite a hefty thumbnail) of exactly what was happening in that very parish. How much were the labourers paid? What equipment was used on the farms? What crops were grown? What factories existed? You will even find that the minister (and incidentally the quality of the reporting varies considerably with the ability and dedication of individual clergymen) was asked to list the worthies and famous men born in the parish. Values change, and the famous men listed in 1790 are not necessarily the ones who are known now. You may even find that someone whom you considered an unknown ancestor was in fact a famous ancestor.

We did when we came to look up the parish of Cramond and found that my wife's grandfather had not been the first to go to Ireland from Scotland – his great-great-great-grandmother's brother had made the trip nearly 200 years earlier and set up the School of Anatomy in Dublin!

And those of you who have reached this page and have still not invested in a PC might like to know that, thanks to the Universities of Glasgow and Edinburgh, the Account can be viewed (and printed off) on a special website.

These then are some titbits to set the intellectual juices flowing. Get along to the nearest reference library and see what it has to offer. You will be surprised.

A DIFFERENT TYPE OF LIBRARY

For purely business reasons, commercial companies have always hung on to their records and these have often proved useful to genealogists. In recent years, however, there has been an upsurge in the maintaining and chronicling of commercial records for historical considerations. More and more companies are employing professional archivists.

My own employers, The Royal Bank of Scotland, for example, had no qualified archivists when *Scottish Roots* was first published and today has four. In the past you needed an ancestor who was in the church, law, medicine or the armed forces to get some real flesh and blood on the skeleton details given by the records. Today, there is a much greater chance of getting information about that ancestor who was a shipping clerk, a banker, an engineer or a printer from the company that employed him.

I'll finish with an experience related to libraries but really about the importance of playing detective whenever possible. It's always fun and it sometimes works.

I was getting frustrated at my inability to find the birthplace of one William Clark Cowie. That key fact was missing from the potted biography of him for my book, *Other Men's Heroes*, which covered 65 Scots honoured on other countries' postage stamps. As he was the first to achieve this accolade, he had been thoroughly investigated by others, but no one had managed to discover his birthplace.

Waiting for a document on an entirely different subject to be delivered to my seat at a reference library, I suddenly thought that he might have written a book. I rushed through the great microfiche catalogue of the British Library and there, sure enough, was his name. He had edited an English-Sulu-Malay dictionary. Back in my Midlothian village, I ordered a copy on the Inter-Library system producing in theory any book held anywhere in Britain. To my surprise, one turned up. The content was of little value with no pointers to the editor's origins. But I noticed that the only copy in Britain outside the British Library was signed by Cowie and had come from Arbroath. There must be a connection.

I phoned the library and asked if they held anything on William Clark Cowie. The following day, the librarian phoned me back. 'We have nothing on your man.'

I was disappointed. 'But he did come home for his father's funeral!' That cracked it. Full details of his well-kent father, an easy steer to his OPR birth entry and all just in time to add a couple of paragraphs to my book.

I make no excuse for repeating: luck needs a lot of work.

ELEVEN

Out and About On Location

A visit to the places where your ancestors lived and worked can have a lot to offer the genealogist.

When researching this book, I walked with my twin sons, Steve and Kevin, down Carrubbers Close, a narrow alleyway opening off Edinburgh's Royal Mile, just down the hill from the Old Tron Kirk.

Steve and Kevin were born in 1966. Their great-great-great-great-grandmother, Anne Dundas, was born two hundred years earlier in 1766. (Incidentally, a good case for the old rule-of-thumb 33 years to a generation.) Carrubbers Close was the narrow access to the congested housing where Anne and her husband, shoemaker James Balbirnie, lived out the last few decades of their lives – both of them passing their eightieth birthday. Anne worked as a sicknurse and it was from this Close that she operated during the cholera epidemic of 1832 which swept along the High Street, killing 600 people in six months, including some from the buildings where Anne and James lived.

A visit to an actual location such as this – and you are not always lucky enough to find the location even remotely reminiscent of the conditions of 150 years ago – can do a lot, not perhaps to add to your totting up of ancestral names but certainly to your understanding of the conditions in which your ancestors lived and worked. The Close has, believe it or not, been considerably widened since the days when the area between North Bridge and the Netherbow was one of the most congested habitations in Europe. Nevertheless, a visit can do more than a book or an engraving to take you back to those days and those settings.

With more and more of your ancestors emerging and coming to life, it is only natural that you too will want to see the places in which all those Births, Marriages and Deaths were taking place. Some of you may be lucky enough to live close at hand; for others it will mean a trip of some distance and even call for a hefty outlay for travel and board. Is it worth it? What can you possibly get out of a visit that couldn't be collected more conveniently from books and records?

The answers to those questions will vary considerably with individual cases and may even depend on your own powers of imagination! You don't have to be Thomas Gray in the churchyard at Stoke Poges or Oliver Goldsmith confronted by the Deserted Village to find that stones and structures, scenes and settings can tell you as much as books and records about the life of your forebears.

You will by this stage have acquired a wealth of detail as far as addresses and occupations are concerned. If these are centred mainly in rural areas, that old Ordnance Survey map which I advised at the beginning will now come into its own, while if your targets are more in Scotland's towns and cities, you will need an up-to-date – or better still out-of-date – street map.

HOMES AND HOUSES

The chances of finding the actual houses in which your family lived a century ago will again vary from one case to the next, but one fortunate by-product of Scotland's poor housing record and high proportion of old housing stock is the existence, in varying degrees of maintenance, of a higher proportion of old houses than you will find in some of the more opulent and favoured areas of the United Kingdom.

It is worth emphasising that the sooner you start, the better chance you have of finding the houses. I came to Scotland in 1970 and it took a few years before we got down to the business of tracking down my wife's Scottish ancestors. Key addresses for the 1840-60 period lay in the old Dumbiedykes area of Edinburgh. I arrived, complete with camera, to find that the two addresses which figure on our family tree had been demolished only a year previously – and there was a bulldozer actually at work on the block where an army-pensioner great-great-uncle was a janitor in 1881.

Let's imagine that you are very lucky and some of the homes are still standing. They will almost certainly have been updated and restructured to some extent, but they will still be worth a photograph – not just of the house itself, but also of the street and any features (a church, a factory) which might have survived from the time your ancestors lived there. I have always found it diplomatic to ask permission of any people living in the house at the present time. After all, just imagine looking out of the window of your own lounge and seeing someone clicking away at your frontage. The courteous act may even bring in a few bonuses about number of rooms, when the extensions were made and so on.

The arrival of the camcorder to which I have already referred gives you another tool with which to record the images of your heritage. The same principles apply – and imagination is going to be much more useful than the specifications of the equipment.

PHOTOGRAPHS

A slight digression on the subject of photographs. The material you are assembling is not just for yourself and not just for the present moment. It is therefore advisable to think big and think long. Go for the best as far as quality is concerned. While instantly available photographs and such like have very great attractions, especially for the impatient, there are other considerations.

If you are putting together a portfolio of illustrations of houses and settings, you are concerned not with immediate delivery, but with two elements – quality and ease of reproduction – which are not the strongest points of the print-in-seconds cameras. Be patient, aim for good colour negatives and you have a source of photographs which will do full justice to the work you have put into the rest of the subject – and which can be reproduced for other members of the family.

There is one piece of modern camera technology that also needs a mention. Digital cameras, while not yet up to the quality of conventional cameras of a similar price, have many advantages, not least the ability to feed your images directly into your PC at home, to view them on your TV screen or to transmit them around the globe via the internet. I know of two delighted new parents who delivered pictures of the first-born to relatives in Vancouver and Sydney before the day was out! The same facility can apply just as well to interchange of images of long-gone members of the family.

Back to the business in hand. You may, of course, not be lucky enough to find intact and charming the cottage where your great-great-grandparents lived or the mill where the man of the house toiled. But, as we have seen, there are other subjects to be photographed. You may not be able to photograph the cottage, but what about the view from the front door? The street in which the house existed? The church? The river? The bridge? There are a hundred-and-one elements which played a part in the life of that family, some of which may still be standing there waiting to be photographed.

There are two buildings which call for particular attention, the church and the local library. By the very nature of your records, the church will have played a central part in the baptisms, weddings and funerals which you have logged *ad infinitum*.

Churches have been more carefully conserved than ordinary dwelling houses. It is much more likely that you will find the church where a couple were married in 1850, 1800 or even 1750 than the building where they set up house. So visit the church and get your photographs taken: the porch where the couple stood after the wedding, the font which came a little later, and do not, of course, neglect that greatest of assets to the genealogist, the graveyards.

There is, paradoxically, something living about a gravestone which means so much more than the bare record of an interment. The task calls for plodding and patience and good waterproof shoes. But persevere – and don't just look for your own family's gravestones. You'll be astonished at just what you can pick up from the others, especially in the small rural areas where the farming families were compact and interlinked. I once went to photograph my grandfather's gravestone, got lost and found *his* father's – a stone whose existence had not been known to any of his present descendants.

Those transcriptions of monumental inscriptions which I described earlier can help you decide whether or not the visit to the graveyards will be worthwhile. They may even help you decipher inscriptions which are now worn away but which a decade or so ago were clear enough.

If you are fortunate enough to find gravestones, take care with the photography. A little brush would not come amiss and, more effective still, try and choose your moment when a low and slanting sun makes the most of any faded lettering. I have also seen effective rubbings taken of gravestones using soft white paper and black heelball in the same way as brass rubbings are made.

When you are out on safari, the local library is one source of valuable information which is quite easy to overlook. It is unlikely that it will be bristling with volumes to the same extent as the large central reference library, but it will make up for any disadvantage in size in its specialisation in the area you are interested in. This will not just manifest itself in the obvious way with such items as files of local newspapers. It may also be reflected in small publications or essays by, say, the local history club. The small local library will also be able to tip you off on any exhibitions or museums in the area which are worth visiting.

TWELVE

The Museums of Scotland

Scotland's new folk museums – time machines that can take you back into the lives of your ancestors.

When we moved into a house in Gorebridge in 1976, we came across a strange object in the garden. Heavy enough to pose problems to a small child, weird in shape, puzzling in consistency, it appeared to be either porous stone or fossilized wood. The weathering had had an effect and its surface was losing a former smoothness. A knowing visitor put us right. 'It's the vertebra of a large whale.' And that was that. Why anyone would want a spinal cotton reel, no matter how imposing, did not seem a worthwhile question to ask, but a year later we got the answer.

Visiting the delightful folk museum in Lewis which owed its origin to the enthusiastic school children of Shawbost, we saw not one but two of our vertebrae! And a placard told us just what they were used for – not as some early Barbara Hepworth to decorate a whaler's cottage (there was no room for such frivolity as that) but for the more mundane function of providing stools for the young children!

This simple and perhaps insignificant fact emerged from one of Scotland's new wave of folk museums which can take you back, in a way very few books or films can, into the lives of your ancestors. By now you will have traced quite a number of forebears and will quite naturally have wanted to progress from knowing when they lived and who they married, how many children they had and what they died of, to wanting to try and share in their existence, to know something of the style and quality of their life rather than its duration, about the places in which the family lived and worked, ate and slept.

The museums which concentrate on social history have developed naturally as our attitudes to history itself have changed. We are now no longer satisfied with tales of treaties and triumphs, dynasties and politics. As a result, there are now throughout Scotland a number of specialised museums where you can turn back the centuries and pitch yourself into the lives of your ancestors, whether they lived (or worked) in a grand house in Edinburgh's New Town, a black house in the far north, a fishing cottage in Fife or a miner's cottage in Dalkeith. The fisherman and the farmer, the cobbler and the miner, the weaver and the fireman, the fishmonger and the carter – all are catered for in Scotland's developing network of 'roots' museums.

For the PC owner, nothing could be simpler than to tap into this network and locate which museum is in the area your ancestors lived, or dedicated to the craft or profession they followed.

www.scottishmuseums.org.uk, the Scottish Museums Council website, lists some 300 museums and galleries throughout Scotland. You can check through these alphabetically or by area. Just clicking on the right part of the map of Scotland will show you immediately which museums cover that area.

Let's take the Kingdom of Fife as an example. Perhaps one of the most diverse counties of Scotland, it has a varied span of industries, from coal to damask, from linoleum to fishing.

The Scottish Museums site lists some twenty museums, nearly half of them with their own websites. A quick run through the profiles and you will find one or two with no real family history dimension, but most will have an attraction to some ancestor-hunters. If your forebears lived in Buckhaven, Burntisland, Crail, Dollar, Dunfermline or Kirkcaldy, you'll be attracted by the local museums there. For a wider picture, the main Fife Folk Museum at Ceres or the Scottish Fisheries Museum at Anstruther are the Kingdom's star attractions. There are some specialist museums covering such topics as emigration, costumes and scientific instruments. The McDouall Stuart Museum at Kirkcaldy offers little of interest for anyone seeking to get into the skin of their Fife ancestors, but will intrigue any Australian visitors. It highlights the exploits of the explorer born in the house, certainly not the first man to try, but indisputably the first to succeed in crossing Australia.

This is a very representative sample of the rich variety of information you will find on this site for whichever area of Scotland that interests you.

Alternatively, a flick through the A-Z list for the whole of Scotland will locate any specialist themes.

There are good links to those museums which have their own websites and that will give you a more precise picture of what to expect there – and can even take you down to such details as opening hours, admission charges and wheelchair accessibility!

Here is a selection, far from comprehensive, which will give you some idea of what to expect. But remember: these are being added to each year!

THE CITIES

Statistics and laws of probability will suggest that very many of you will, in the nineteenth century at least, find that your forebears are earning their crusts in one of what are now Scotland's five cities. This is good news, because these naturally are the very places where museums and archives are well established and well funded. What you find will naturally reflect the very different characteristics of those five cities and here is a rundown on what you might look out for.

Edinburgh

The capital city is rich in 'time machines', but Edinburgh life down the ages is probably best portrayed in the **Museum of Edinburgh** in the Canongate. It houses a comprehensive display in one of Europe's most historic and atmospheric streets.

In the finest Adam town square of all, Edinburgh's Charlotte Square, **The Georgian House** is among the city's top tourist attractions. From the elegant drawing room to the fascinating kitchen, the whole building is decked out in the style of 1800, even down to removing many of the Victorian 'improvements'. While it is typically Edinburgh, it does at the same time represent a standard which the landed gentry around Scotland would be attempting to emulate – and as such will provide as much of an insight into their lives as to those of the capital's aristocracy.

Across the valley, brooding on the rocky ridge from the Castle to the Palace, lies the Old Town of Edinburgh and it too has acquired a fine and worthy counterpart to the Georgian House in the beautifully transformed **Gladstone's Land**, a six-storey tenement in the Lawnmarket. The house was built in 1620 and has now been restored to the style of that period. Once again, this typically Edinburgh setting will also help stir the imaginations of those whose roots lie in other large Scottish towns among the houses of the merchants.

Glasgow

Scotland's largest city has its museum of local history in the **People's Palace**, opened in 1898 and telling the story of Glasgow from 1175 onwards – although strongest in the period where your ancestor-hunting will have concentrated. Important collections relating to the tobacco and other industries, stained glass, ceramics, political and social movements including temperance, co-operatives, suffragettes, and socialism. Photographs, film sequences and reminiscences to satisfy the most demanding Glasgwegian.

Glasgow's answer to Edinburgh's Gladstone's Land is **Provand's Lordship**, the oldest house in the city, built before Columbus had gathered together enough cash to go west, now an impressive museum with seventeenth-century furniture.

Throughout its history, **Barony Chambers** has been at different times a town hall, council chambers and court room, jail and school. Now a museum, it illustrates the social and industrial history of the Kirkintilloch district. A reconstructed single end and wash house give a vivid picture of early twentieth-century working-class life. Iron founding, coal mining, weaving and boat building are described in displays of photographs, tools and equipment. There are also displays on the Forth and Clyde Canal.

Clydebank Museum is situated beside the shipyard where many of the famous liners of the Clyde were built. The museum collections include local, social and industrial history artefacts relating to life in Clydebank both past and present and to shipbuilding and engineering in a town which became world famous for building ships.

Dundee

To get an overall feel for Dundee life, you really need to see the **McManus Galleries** at Albert Square, Tayside's major regional museum and art gallery.

To get an insight into the city's unique specialisation, go and see **Verdant Works** – a working jute mill, the story of a city, its people and the industry that made it. With a stunning range of displays including film shows, interactive computers and original machinery lovingly restored to working condition, Verdant Works brings to life an industry which imported its raw material from India, processed it and sold it to power the world's sailing ships and, incidentally, covered the wagons that won the Wild West.

Aberdeen

Gladstone's Land and Provand's Lordship are matched by **Provost Skene's House** where a merchant lived in the seventeenth century, a time when Aberdeen was emerging as a flourishing trading port. It is now an attractive period museum with elegantly furnished rooms from the seventeenth, eighteenth and nineteenth centuries. Don't miss the costume gallery with its monthly exhibitions of fashion through the ages, or the changing exhibitions of Aberdeen's social history in the attic. Get a slightly different angle at **James Dun's House** – an eighteenth-century town house renovated for use as a museum with permanent displays and special exhibitions.

The **Maritime Museum** not only covers the city's historic traditions, it brings them up to date by letting you see what it is like to live and work on a massive oil platform in the middle of the North Sea. Using models, real equipment and computer displays, the exhibitions bring the North Sea experience to life.

Inverness

The latest and not least proud of Scotland's citites is perhaps representative of a far greater hinterland than any of the others.

TOWNS AND VILLAGES

The Scottish towns have never lagged behind the cities in fierce civic pride and a feeling for heritage, so you will not be surprised to find that few, if any, have neglected to display their traditions and way of life. You saw from the list of Fife museums that you can almost guarantee that wherever your ancestors lived, worked or went to market there will now be a display to help you share in their way of life. The villages invariably reflect the economic activity of the area, the fishing or farming, mining or trade, and you will see later that they are represented by the museums which focus on such activities.

THE HIGHLANDS

Despite the sparse population, the Highlands will have supplied ancestors out of all proportion to any initial mathematical estimate. Throughout history, the surplus population had left the homelands in search of at best a fortune or at worst a living. Political pressures, a penchant for trade and an equally marketable facility for warfare had often sent them further afield and in the industrial explosion of the eighteenth and nineteenth centuries, many were sucked into the Central Belt of Scotland and the manufacturing areas south of the Border.

As a result, many of you will find that your Scottish roots, at first traced to the populous Central Belt, in fact go deeper to the communities beyond the Helensburgh to Stonehaven line.

You will have no difficulty in gaining an understanding of those communities from today's folk museums. Here are some of the best.

If you can only take in one of these fascinating centres try the **Highland Folk Museum** at Kingussie, an open air complex which you can visit all the year round. It is situated on the main Perth–Inverness road, about twelve miles south west of Aviemore. It includes an eighteenth-century shooting lodge, a black house from Lewis, a clack mill and exhibits of farming equipment. Inside you'll find displays including a barn, a dairy, a stable and an exhibition illustrating the life of Highland tinkers. And if you want to see just what your Highland ancestors wore, fought with, sat on or played with, this is for you.

Very many Scots in North America, Australia and New Zealand will trace their roots back to Caithness and Sutherland, the scene of so many clearances. At Caithness, on the A9 between Helmsdale and Wick, **Laidhay Caithness Croft**, open from Easter to September, will show just what sort of life those Scots were leaving. An early eighteenth-century croft complex has been conserved complete with stable house and byre under a single thatched roof. The complex is furnished throughout in the furniture of the period.

You'll find a particular delight at Strathpeffer – the **Museum of Highland Childhood**. Located in a restored Victorian station, it uses evocative photographs, an award-winning video and displays interpreting life at home, on the land and at school. The dolls, toys and costumes alone are worth the trip.

THE ISLANDS – TO THE WEST

Although often lumped in with for the Highlands for administrative convenience, the islands of Scotland have their own distinctive heritages. Again, you will be hard pressed to find an ancestral island which won't satisfy your quest for enlightenment.

Isle of Lewis – Lewis has two particularly important points to visit if you are to get a feel for the lives of the crofters and fishermen. An evocative black house at Arnol, constructed without mortar and roofed with thatch, shows a central peat fire and a number of authentic furnishings. Not far away is the superb Shawbost Museum where I found my whalebone stools – begun by the local school children and expanded into a higgledy-piggledy collection of the minutiae of crofting life.

The Cumbraes – Garrison House in Millport houses the Museum of the Cumbraes, particularly strong on Victorian and Edwardian times when the islands were an integral part of the cruising holiday scene in the West of Scotland.

Skye – Perhaps the most evocative name in the Scottish islands, Skye too has its black house and water mill, to the west of Dunvegan. A feature of the crofter's house is a replica whisky still! Kilmuir Croft Museum north of Portree has exhibits which include a wall bed and an array of domestic and farming implements.

Mull – Just south of Dervaig, an attractive stone-built byre has been converted to provide a museum of crofting life on Mull, using lifelike figures and a sound commentary.

Other island museums include: the **Bute** Museum at Rothesay, the **South Uist** Folk Museum, housed in a traditional thatched cottage, and the Museum of **Islay** Life established in an old Victorian United Free Church building.

THE ISLANDS – TO THE NORTH

Shetland – There is a fine croft house at Dunrossness, 25 miles south of Lerwick, where a complete thatched croft complex has been carefully restored with a mid-nineteenth-century thatched croft house and steading, complete with contemporary furnishings. A water mill nearby is worth a visit. Supplement the impact of the croft house with a visit to the fine museum open all year round at Lower Hillhead in Lerwick. It has four galleries, dealing with archaeology, art and textiles, folk life and shipping.

Orkney – The Kirbuster Museum will go back further than any family tree, with the unique survival in Northern Europe of a traditional rural dwelling with central hearth and stone bed. There is an eighteenth-century extension with parlour and bedrooms. The extensive grounds, bordered by the Burn of Kirbuster, include farm buildings and machinery, crop growing and livestock. There is a Victorian garden and a putting green.

In most instances, the local displays will cover the activities of your ancestors, but there are specialist museums which might be able to focus more sharply on an ancestor's trade or profession.

AGRICULTURE

Fife – The Fife Folk Museum at Ceres has a fine setting in an old seventeenth-century weigh house near an old bridge in an attractive village. It concentrates on the agricultural and domestic past of Fife life. And don't omit to walk to the nearby church and see the horseshoe gallery.

The Borders – the Hirsel Homestead Museum near Coldstream is housed on the estate of the Home family. It contains forestry equipment, gardening implements, laundry equipment and general farm implements.

DOWN TO THE SEA IN SHIPS

With her clusters of islands and seemingly infinite coastline, Scotland (and your ancestors) could never get far away from the business of fishing and all its allied trades. The following reflect the relationship:

Fishing – Scottish Fisheries Museum at Anstruther Harbour, in St Ayle's Land, a building with a charter dated 1318, houses a fascinating collection of items illustrating the fisherman's life at home and at sea, historical and modern. The museum also contains a marine aquarium and is restoring a 70-ft sailing 'Fifie'. At the east pier in the same village you can go aboard the North Carr Lightship – a floating museum and well worth a visit.

Buckie on the Moray Firth has a maritime museum which shows clothing, gear and models relating to the fishing industry. Interestingly, the Anson gallery houses a collection of watercolours on the development of fishing in Scotland. Further along the Moray Firth, Nairn Fishertown Museum has a collection of articles and photographs connected with the fishing heritage of the area, and with herring fishing industries during the steam drifter era. It has good coverage too of the domestic life of the fisher folk.

Whales – Peterhead's Arbuthnot Museum covers the development of fishing and whaling and has a large number of Arctic exhibits. And, to show that not even museums have to dwell on the past, it has a section on offshore oil as befits one of Scotland's major beneficiaries of North Sea activity.

Dundee was also an important whaling base and the Broughty Castle museum reflects this past with harpoons, darts, knives, axes and scrimshaws galore. The good ship *Discovery* is now back at its home. It was, of course, like many polar exploration vessels, a whaler in her early years, although the splendid exhibit there is concerned mainly with her voyages to the Antarctic.

Lighthouses – Kinnaird Head was the first lighthouse to be built by the Northern Lighthouse Board in 1787 and the only lighthouse to be built on top of a fortified castle. In 1824, the lighthouse was reconstructed inside Kinnaird Castle by Robert Stevenson, engineer to the Northern Lighthouse Board. Decommissioned in 1991, and maintained for the nation, with the help of Historic Scotland and Scotland's Lighthouse Museum Trust, the original lighthouse and engine room are now preserved as they were the day the last keeper left. The Museum of Scottish Lighthouses boasts the largest and best collection of lighthouse lenses and equipment in the UK, plus a multi-screen audio visual which tells the story of the lighthouse service in Scotland.

You can also learn something of the life and work of the many Scots who manned the lighthouses in Arbroath's Signal Tower.

TOWN TRADES

The trades of the towns are well displayed at Biggar, in the Gladstone Court Street Museum. This is in the unique form of an 'indoor' street museum of shops and windows. Grocer, photographer, dressmaker, bank, school, library, ironmonger, chemist, china merchant and telephone exchange are featured. An open-air museum is being developed and a seventeenth-century farmhouse rebuilt. A reconstructed Edwardian shop also figures at Kirkcaldy's Museum. At Fochabers in the north-east, Old Baxter's shop offers a similar chance to step back into the past.

Shoemaking was, in view of the difficulty in automating such an essential industry, a trade followed by many. There were, for example, at the time of the 1851 Census well over 30,000 shoemakers cobblers in Scotland! The fact that Burns immortalised one of these – Souter Johnnie in 'Tam o' Shanter' – has been instrumental in giving the shoemakers a museum of their own. Souter Johnnie's House in Kirkoswald, not far from Maybole, is a thatched cottage which was the home of village cobbler (souter) John Davidson at the end of the eighteenth century. The cottage now contains a selection of Burnsiana – and an exhibition of the contemporary tools of the cobbler's craft.

DIGGING FOR A LIVING

Scotland's mining and extractive industries developed early – and many of you may have traced back your roots to areas where these hard and demanding jobs were concentrated. After being ignored for a very long time, these industries are now receiving some long overdue historical attention.

Centuries of coal – Of all the materials hewn from the crust of Scotland, coal has probably involved more of your ancestors, spread over a greater part of the country than any other. The museums of the industry are housed at Prestongrange in East Lothian, only eight miles east of Edinburgh, and Newtongrange, a similar distance to the south. On the site of a colliery with 800 years of recorded running history (just think about that!), the museum has an impressive centrepiece in the form of an 1874 Cornish Beam Pumping Engine and its five-floor engine house. The former power house is now an exhibition hall with many mining artefacts, plans, photographs and documents. There are also two steam locomotives, a hundred-year-old steam navvy and a colliery winding machine on site.

(You will also find areas devoted to coal miners in the museums of Kirkcaldy and Blantyre, the latter the Livingstone National Memorial).

Iron, coal and bricks – the Dunaskin Open Air Museum in East Ayrshire tells a very different story of the county from the usual Burns associations. The Industrial Revolution's ironworking, coal mining and brick making is brought to life with audio-visual presentations, industrial machinery and a period cottage.

Slate quarrying – Along with North Wales, the north-west coast of Scotland was one of the centres to provide slate for the great house-building projects of the nineteenth century. Easdale was the centre of the industry and the Easdale Island Museum, set among the quarrymen's houses, contains photographs, records and artefacts. The Glencoe and North Lorn Museum in Glencoe village deals with the famous local industry as well as with the more romantic activities of Bonnie Prince Charlie. The museum is housed in a number of thatched cottages.

Swinging the lead – Lead was another valuable raw material found in Scotland and localised to a large extent around Wanlockhead, Scotland's highest village. The Museum of the Scottish Lead Mining Industry is there, bristling with mining and social relics housed in a cottage. In the open-air section, you'll find a lead mine beam engine, smelt and but-and-ben cottages. You can even take a guided tour down a lead mine and see conditions at first hand. And if you have tracked your ancestors back to the lead industry, there's a local library with books and records of the reading society which was founded in 1756.

Paraffin – In the 1970s the oil industry returned after a long spell away from home to the country where it all started. If your ancestors came from Pumpherston, West Calder, Winchburgh, Broxburn or Bathgate, they may very well have played a part in James 'Paraffin' Young's empire. Get along to the Almondvale Heritage Centre to learn more.

A SCOTTISH SOLDIER OR TWO

Fighting has always been a major Scottish industry, with the nation providing over the centuries quality fighters not only to Britain but also to a strange mix of foreign powers. At home, the fighting tradition has been firmly built on the great Scottish regiments. While the reader who traces ancestors who were professional soldiers may well have to go to London to find the details of an individual, it is to Scotland that he must look to learn something of the regiments with which his forebear fought.

Argyle and Sutherland Highlanders – The setting of Stirling Castle will take some beating – this fine regiment museum does full justice to it, particularly strong in its medal collection.

Black Watch – This famous regiment has its headquarters and museum in Balhousie Castle in Perth. The exhibits offer a dramatic way of following the development of the regiment from 1740 to the present day.

The Cameronians – The Cameronians (Scottish Rifles)

Regimental Museum is in Hamilton and, in addition to the usual regimental exhibits, is especially strong on the Covenanting times.

Gordon Highlanders – The regimental headquarters in Aberdeen is open all the year round and offers fine displays relating to the Gordon Highlanders' varied campaigns. There are collections of uniforms, colours and banners, silver and medals and a library with historical material and photograph albums

Queen's Own Highlanders – Fort George, near Inverness, was begun in 1748 as a result of the fright caused by the 1745 Jacobite Rising, and is one of Europe's finest late artillery fortifications. It houses the museum of the Queen's Own Highlanders.

Royal Scots – The Royal Scots have their museum at Edinburgh Castle. An impressive display of pictures, badges, brassware and other historical relics of the regiment awaits you.

Royal Highland Fusiliers – Glasgow is the base for the regiment in which are concentrated the traditions of the Royal Scots Fusiliers, The Highland Light Infantry and the Royal Highland Fusiliers.

The Scottish Horse Museum – Scottish Horse was a yeomanry regiment and at the Cross, Dunkeld, you will find exhibits, uniforms, photographs, maps and, most significantly for the ancestor-hunter, rolls of all those who served in Scottish Horse.

The Scottish United Services Museum – Edinburgh Castle houses the greatest of the military museums – easy to get at and comprehensive in the extreme.

Don't forget the sailors – in Dundee. The oldest British-built warship still afloat, *HMS Unicorn* was launched in 1824. It portrays the flavour of life in the Royal Navy during the golden age of sail.

DISTILLING

Ask a hundred tourists to name a Scottish industry – and distilling will almost certainly come to mind in the majority of cases. It was never an industry which employed vast numbers of Scots (but it is worth remembering that there were many ancillary trades from coopers to coppersmiths that may have been pursued by your forebears). It is, however, an industry which is well displayed. You will find actual working distilleries open and welcoming, and eager to display some of the secrets of the art and mystery. **Dufftown's** own museum deals with the vital Banffshire industry and from there you can follow the Whisky Trail and take in a number of famous distilleries including Glendronach, Glenfardas, Glenfiddich, Glen Grant, Glenlivet, and at Keith the oldest of them all, Strathisla. Off the main Banffshire trail, you'll find other distilleries well worth a visit, especially in the islands. Look out for them.

THE TEXTILE INDUSTRIES

Barely a corner of Scotland was without its spinning and weaving activity and specialisation – and it would be quite difficult to get back to the eighteenth century without coming across at least one forebear 'in the business'.

New Lanark – Perhaps the finest example of Scotland's preserved industrial past is at New Lanark, the setting of Robert Owen's advanced experiments in establishing a model manufacturing community. This is one of the must-sees of Scotland's museums, although that word museum does little justice to this benchmark for bringing history to life.

Handloom weaving – If you get back as far as the eighteenth century, your forebears would certainly have been doing their weaving by hand in a cottage. At Kilbarchan, west of Paisley, a cottage has been preserved as a home typical of the period when Kilbarchan was a thriving centre of hand-loom weaving.

Linen and damask – The weaving of fine linen and damask objects was the specialisation which made Dunfermline industry famous. It is naturally well represented in the town museum. Kinross, not too far up the road, also has a section on linen manufacture in its museum.

Cotton spinning – One of the many aspects of the local area's activity on display in Blantyre's Livingstone National Memorial is cotton spinning.

Spinning and weaving by hand – Over on the west coast, on the southern edge of Oban, you can see at McDonald's Mill an exhibition of the story of spinning and weaving, and actual demonstrations of how these types were done by hand.

Paisley wear – Scottish Paisley design has found its way to all corners of the world, and the industry is well displayed at the Paisley Museum with lots of superb shawls.

TRANSPORTS OF DELIGHT

In the nineteenth century, which will take up much of your family research, transport was a major activity in Scotland – not just using it, but laying the foundations for it, building the equipment, and, of course, running it.

Transport in general – The Daddy of them all is of course the great Glasgow Museum of Transport – the history of transport on land and sea with vehicles from horse-drawn carriages to motorcycles, fire engines, railway engines and motor cars (including the oldest in Scotland). The Clyde Room has ship models plus there is a reconstruction of a 1938 Glasgow street and a replica underground station.

Canals – When the Union Canal was opened in 1822, part of its infrastructure involved a large stable block (to keep the horse-power happy) at Linlithgow. Today, those stables house records, photographs, an audio-visual display and relics of the history of the canal (not forgetting a lot of the wildlife around it). You can also go on a trip by canal boat (Ratho and Linlithgow) to get the feel of one of the wonders of the early nineteenth century. Grangemouth Museum also concentrates on the canals of central Scotland, including canal tools and a model lock, plus exhibits relating to the *Charlotte Dundas,* the world's first practical steamship.

Railways – In addition to the great museums of Glasgow and Edinburgh whose working models and actual exhibits have fascinated small boys of all ages for generations, the Scottish Railway Preservation Society, based at Bo'ness near Falkirk, offers a fine display of restored railway vehicles. If you want to experience travel on a steam-engine you can do so there or on private lines at Strathspey, Lochty and Alford.

PROFESSIONS

The professions are strangely reticent in the proliferation of roots displays.

But if you're in Edinburgh, a visit to the law courts, the gruesome museum in Surgeons Hall and the Bank of

Scotland's exhibit on the Mound might help you understand the day-to-day activities of any lawyers, surgeons or bankers in your family tree.

SERVING THE COMMUNITY

The host of local authority services which now influence our lives at so many stages are comparatively new – and the people employed in them equally short on heritage, but you may be surprised to find that there are in Scotland museums to give you something of the background to:

Policemen – At the Strathclyde Police Headquarters in Glasgow, there is a small police museum showing the history of the police service in Scotland – along with some articles from a variety of crime cases!

Firemen - As befits the city which 'invented' the municipal firefighting force, Edinburgh has a museum complete with old uniforms, equipment and engines. This is one business where demands cannot be predicted in advance so there may be times when you can't see around as everyone is out fighting fires. The museum is named the Braidwood and Rushbrook Fire Museum. Braidwood, having set up the first Fire Brigade in the 1820s, then went off to London to show them it could be done there too.

Prison-officers – On the site of Jedburgh Castle a modern 'reform' jail was built in 1825. Rooms have been interestingly reconstructed to recreate the 'reformed' system of the early nineteenth century. It should interest you, whether your forebears were here as workers or as prisoners! There's competition on the other side of Scotland at Inveraray where a Scottish Tourist Board four-star attraction delivers imaginative exhibitions, a magnificent 1820 courtroom and two prisons, with guides in period costume. You can listen to trials in the courtroom equipped with induction loop for the hard of hearing. Follow up the sentence with a visit to the prison.

Social workers – Scotland has in the Heatherbank Museum of Social Services near Glasgow what could be the world's only museum dedicated to that subject. There are exhibitions, 2,500 slides of the nineteenth and early twentieth centuries and 5,000 volumes in the reference library! Again, whether your forebears gave out the charity or received it, this has potential.

SERVICE DOWNSTAIRS

While the stately homes of Scotland – and there are many of them, distributed all over the country – might seem to be target only for those of you with stately ancestors, it is worth remembering that there were usually far more people working below stairs, in the gardens and the stables than in the family itself. The mansion house is as relevant to them as it is to the owners. One might even argue it is more relevant, as so few of them got the chance to leave it. If your ancestors were chambermaids or valets, gardeners or grooms, you can see just where they worked. And there is a always a fascination in these grand houses with the kitchens and mechanics of preparing meals.

THE CLAN MUSEUMS

Perhaps the image of Scotland which gets the most airing on the international scene is the picture of a rigid, clan-orientated society all living, if we are to believe those maps and tea-towels, in clearly defined 'reservations'. The truth is far from that, but the existence of the clans was a very real element in the lives of your ancestors Highland –

and you may gain an insight into the times from a visit to some of the relevant clan museums. Here is a selection:

Clan Donald Centre – Based at Armadale Castle, the centre houses a museum of the history of the Macdonalds and the Lords of the Isles. The setting is particularly beautiful.

Clan Donnachaidh Museum – The Clan takes in Reid, Robertson, MacConnachie, Duncan, MacInroy and others – which is a fair chunk of Scots. The museum is particularly strong on items associated with the Jacobite Risings of 1715 and 1745, and is to be found four miles west of Blair Atholl.

Clan Gunn Museum – The museum is located in the mid-eighteenth-century parish church of Latheron on the A9, before it reaches Wick.

Clan Macpherson Museum – The clan museum has a range of relics and memorials including the black chanter, green banner and charmed sword, Princes Charles Edward Stuart relics and a magnificent silver centrepiece. You'll find it at Newtonmore, 15 miles south of Aviemore.

Strathnaver Museum – While this is not specifically a clan museum, it is right in the heart of the Clan Mackay country and is associated with the Sutherland Clearances with which many overseas Scots may well be able to establish links.

LOCAL LINKS

In addition to professions and trades, regiments and industries, you will have placed your forebears within precise locations within Scotland – and this means that the local museums will have a great deal to offer in terms of telling you about the life of the community in which your forebears lived. There are too many first-rate museums to list them all, but you should see if the area you are focusing on is covered by any of the local museums. For those without a PC or as a taster for those who have one, here is a selection.

Banff, Banchory (a small display in the old Council Chambers), **Bo'ness** (especially strong on the local manufactures of pottery, cast-iron and salt-pan implements), **Brechin** (housed in the library), **Burntisland, Coupar Angus, Dingwall** (in the fine eighteenth-century town house, strong on the career of local hero Sir Hector MacDonald), **Dumfries** (covering the whole of the Solway area, based on a 200-year-old windmill and featuring a camera obscura), **Falkirk** (good on local pottery, clocks, weapons and Victoriana), **Glenesk** (nicely folk-orientated), **Haddington** (a small display, but here the whole town is a museum and evocative of the inhabitants' past), **Hawick** (in Wilton Lodge Park, superb setting, excellent on Border relics plus good art exhibitions), **Inverkeithing, Inverurie** (thematic exhibitions three times a year), **Irvine, Kinross** (good on local peat-cutting and military activities), **Largs** (local history books and photographs), **Paisley, Saltcoats** (excellent on local manufacture of salt and export of coal to Ireland), **Sanquhar, Stonehaven** (fishing in particular, but a fine building too which has served as storehouse, prison and lodging house in its time), **Stewartry** (museum at Kirkcudbright, with the additional interest for any US visitors that the founder of their Navy, John Paul Jones, was born nearby), and **Wigtown** (spotlight on dairy farming and local explorer Sir John Ross).

The museums of Scotland may not do much to satisfy the ancestor-bagger looking for more and more names, but they will take you back to the worlds of those ancestors. They may not add bones to the skeleton. They will certainly add flesh.

THIRTEEN

Doing It From a Distance

An approach to tracking down your Scots ancestors if you can't get to Edinburgh – or even to Scotland.

If Neil Armstrong set something of a record for Scottish wandering, Alan Bean underlined the point by leaving behind on the moon a piece of MacBean tartan. Fictional Scots James T Kirk, 'Bones' McCoy and Scottie may have travelled even further, but it all goes to emphasise the Scots itch to explore.

The result of this and that habit of setting up Caledonian Societies is that there are people from every corner of the world who see themselves as Scottish and their roots as undeniably tartan.

For them, the main theme of this book – the mouth-watering treasures that await them throughout the length and breadth of Scotland, and at the East end of Princes Street, Edinburgh, in particular – may seem a little irrelevant. This chapter is written especially for them – and indeed for many Scots who cannot get down to Edinburgh and devote days or weeks to this ancestor-hunting kick.

Cheer up. The impact of computer and website, CD-ROM and internet has made your task much more streamlined and fascinating than it was just a decade ago. I've already hinted at many of these possibilities, but there are others.

But patience, let's reflect on the fundamentals again before we go for gee-whizzery.

Even if you are doing it from a distance, the principles outlined in this book remain valid.

The first step is to find out as much as possible from

your own sources. Go and read the first chapter again and you will see how to set about amassing the type of information that is even more essential to anyone who is not able to carry out the research in Scotland in person.

In particular, look out for specific and clearly dated links with Scotland.

When did your ancestor leave Scotland? Arrive in your present country? Do you have any records which can help to answer these points?

In addition to the family interviews/letters mentioned in this book, think in particular of the following:

Are there any records in my present country which give details of the Scottish link?

- A will made in Australia by your grandfather may mention brothers and sisters still left in Scotland.

- Scots leaving home in the nineteenth century were not required to file any details here in Scotland. Catching a boat across the ocean was no different, as far as Government records were concerned, from catching a bus today. Records do, however, often exist at the other end. Ships' passenger lists were often filed at the port of entry. Governments often kept records of immigration, which can compensate for Scotland's lack of emigration records.

- Death records of, say, a Scot who came to Canada and died there may carry the name of his parents. If so, this is a very valuable piece of information, along with any details of his place of birth. (These are details which may even have been carried in the immigration records.)

Are there any less formal clues to the Scottish connection?

- Scots often named their house in the new home after a

farm or village or area where they lived in Scotland. Any records of your forebears' first years in their new home may indicate this.

Are there any family traditions which could throw a light on Scotland?

- For the most part, the bulk of family traditions are poor guides to reality, but it is not always the case. Often, an important element is handed down by word of mouth and where the details are precise enough this can be a help.

Are there any documents which bridge the gap between Scotland and the new home?

Books? Diaries? Photographs? Old photographs may not have a background which will enable you to locate the setting, but commercial photographers usually have their mark somewhere on the surround or even back of the print. If an old fading print bears the stamp of, say, 'Macfarlane, Photographer; Crieff', that could provide a pointer to the family origins.

Do you know anything of the family that were left behind?

Let us suppose that your grandfather came from Scotland and died in New Zealand and that his records in New Zealand give no indications of his parents or birthplace in Scotland. Did he have any brothers or sisters who did not go to New Zealand with him? What were their names? Were they older or younger than he was? More importantly, do you have any precise details of when they married? Or when they died? If you knew that his sister Isabella died in Dundee in 1897, that information would enable you to get from the Scottish records the same information as if your grandfather had died there.

Do you know anything of the Church to which your Scots ancestor belonged?

There was usually a tradition of church-going which passed on from parents to children. Particularly when looking back beyond the civil records, it is important to know which church was likely to have kept records of Births, Marriages and Deaths. As I have mentioned, the established Church of Scotland records are the ones kept by the Register-General in his old, pre-1855 material.

What was the profession or trade of your Scots ancestor?

This could provide one of the most valuable guides to tracking down a family (and not only in helping confirm that the Ian Macleod you track down in Scotland is the same one that you knew about in Nova Scotia!). The professions have their own very fine directories, so that if the emigrating Scot was a doctor, minister or lawyer, you have a very good chance of finding him. Similarly, if he attended university in Scotland, it would be handy to see what information is carried on him in the directories of graduates. The same would apply to any school directories which may exist.

It is not only the professions, however, for which there are fine, informative records. The army records housed in London, provided you have some idea of the regiment, can give much information of value to the ancestor-hunter. Moreover, almost every trade or occupation found its way into the directories which cover most of Scotland's cities from the early nineteenth century onwards. So if your ancestor was a bookseller or coachhirer, a bootmaker or a policeman, in Dundee or Glasgow, Edinburgh or Perth, this is invaluable as an aid to tracking him down.

Did the family own any land, no matter how small, in Scotland?

The great Sasine registers list the owners (but not the tenants) of all land in Scotland. If you have a date and an address, it is possible to extract information from the Sasines which could help build up extra information on your family. The main aim of all this activity is to build up as much information as possible on your Scottish links, because the quality and quantity of the information which it is possible to extract from the records depends to a large extent on just what information you start with.

I have extolled the benefits of electronic wizardry to the ancestor-hunter. These have an even more dramatic impact on the readers who are forced to carry out most or even all of their research away from the Scottish records. Let's recap on – or indeed introduce – some of those developments which have brought you, sir, sunning yourself there in Perth, Western Australia, or you, madam, pottering in your garden in Perth, Canada, not to mention you there in Perth on the silvery Tay, right into the research rooms of Edinburgh.

THE INDEXES AT THE GRO

A large proportion of this book has been devoted to the work at GRO. Now, within the last year or two, the indexes which are at the heart of that work have become available, through the web, to researchers anywhere in the world. The indexes which I showed you on the keyboards in New Register House are also at your fingertips in any of the Perths.

The Scots ORIGINS service is to be found at www.origins.net. That will give you a fully searchable index of Scottish Births and Marriages and Deaths, from 1553 to 1899, Deaths from 1855 to 1924 and Census data for 1881, 1891 and

1901. That's more than 30,000,000 entries by the way. (The cut-off dates show that the GRO are providing all this for genealogical research rather then nosey-neighbour satisfaction.)

WHAT DO YOU GET AT ORIGINS?

For the Birth, Marriages and Deaths after 1855, the ORIGINS site indexes will provide full names, spouses' names for marriages, year and registration district and number. For pre-1855 entries, you'll get similar information, but also the name of parents for births (usually but not always), the name of the parish and a more precise date, giving day and month as well as year.

For the 1881, 1891 and 1901 Census, you'll get full name, sex, age and enumeration district. The combination will often help you put together family groups. You can also access household returns direct.

These are only, of course, the indexes. If you were at New Register House you would then set off in search of the microfiche or microfilm to look at the actual entry. But you folk in the Perths cannot do that. If you want to see the entry, you have to order one – you'll see the costs and address at Appendix 1. In many cases you may not need to do this, the details in the index may be enough. But realise that there may be valuable extra information in the entry. The post-1855 will certainly carry much more than the index and even a 1778 birth entry might reveal some details of the parents (father's occupation for example) or the names of the godparents who might be relatives.

It costs £6 (say US$10), payment by credit card, to access ORIGINS. This gives 30 pages to study and/or download and you can visit the site as many times as you wish for 24 hours after your credit card payment is authorised.

THE FAMILYSEARCH LINK TO SALT LAKE CITY

The work on the GRO indexes can be dramatically augmented by the LDS site, FamilySearch. Go back and read chapter six.

THE WORLD WIDE WEB

Again you should re-read the section on the GENUKI site, which will tell you more about the avenues to explore than any other single website

THE CD-ROMS

You can get the index to the 1891 Census through ORIGINS, but just as helpful, perhaps even more so as it goes further back, is the LDS index to the 1881 Census. This is available at all of the LDS centres. But more importantly, it is available for the whole of Scotland, or for Britain if you feel your searches might stray outside Scotland, on a CD-ROM. Full details are on the FamilySearch site and you can order the CD by post or by internet.

1. Ancestors by post

You can build up a wealth of information by ordering, from the Registrar-General, copies of all the key documents which are needed to build up your family tree. This is:

a. *Expensive* – you, unlike the searcher on the spot who can take notes from a record, have to purchase a copy of the document. The charges are reasonable (you'll find them listed in Appendix I) but they mount up.

b. *Slow* – you have to wait for two postal services (you to the Registrar-General, he to you) with a searching and processing time in between. You might console yourself that the Sassenach, banned from the documents themselves, has no real alternative to this one. You usually can't get on with the next stage until you have noted the details carried on the first document.

c. *Dependent on accurate information* – the Registrar-General's staff are not involved in the business of research. They will find for you and copy an entry for which you provide enough information to make its location feasible. If you want a death certificate of George Macrae, who died in Inverness in 1876, they will provide it. If you want a certificate for a George (or was it Graham?) Macrae who died somewhere north of Inverness, between 1870 and 1878, they are less likely to provide it.

Nevertheless, this is a feasible means of setting about the initial research. And it does have the benefit of providing you with copies or photostats of the actual documents which log your ancestors' history.

2. Using the professional searchers

If the staff of the Registrar-General are not in the business of personalised ancestry research, there are others who are – providing the on-the-spot investigation, speeded, one may add, by an expertise and flair for the records which cannot be acquired overnight, for people who want to find out more about their Scottish roots!

I spoke to Stuart Reid of Scottish Roots to get a professional genealogist's view of the service. (The research company Scottish Roots has only a tenuous connection with this book. When Stuart's father Tony was returning to Scotland after a long spell in Brussels and wanted to set up the company, he was taken by the title of the book which had just appeared. He rang and asked if I had any objection to his using the name. I did not.)

How should someone choose a researcher?

Stuart: 'Like any specialist business, it is always a bit of a gamble, but choose one you feel comfortable with. My advice would be firstly to find someone/a company who has been in the business for at least seven years, reflecting a degree of experience at the record office, and also competence in running a business.

'There are no formal qualifications as such. Scottish Roots, for example, employ researchers who show experience, diligence, and flair at the record office, rather than academic qualifications. A great detective would not necessarily learn the trade sitting in a classroom!'

How do you set about finding a researcher?

'GRO at New Register House provides a list of professional researchers, though it is at pains to point out that they cannot vouch for their work. Nevertheless, it is a good guide. It is advisable to stay clear of anyone who demands full payment up front, and/or who doesn't provide a full address and phone number. On a practical front it is useful to find researchers who offer credit card facilities.

What do you get for your money, and how far can you go?

'Perhaps the most difficult of all questions, and also variable from one researcher to another. A company such as Scottish Roots offers a package called the Standard Search, and costs around £200. In this category the customer would receive a factual typed report with all details from certificates, parish registers, census returns, along with full reference numbers. In this time one should expect to trace a single line back to the 1780s from, say, a 1940 birth certificate. However, each case is unique with different sets of problems, such as illegitimacy, a widespread name, searching in a parish which kept poor records, etc.'

Has the upsurge in alternative sources, websites, local microfiche reduced business for a professional researcher.
'Yes and no. Whilst it is possible to undertake a degree of research on your own, it is still more productive to spend a few days at the record office because all the records you are likely to need are under one roof.

'The increase in documentation 'on line' has at least made the whole subject of family history more accessible, but it has also created a lot of confusion and frustration. At the end of the day you still need to locate birth, marriage and death certificates. Nevertheless, you can add flesh to the skeleton by finding information at local level and also via the internet. It is therefore advisable to get a professional to undertake the initial heavy spadework.'

The factors that influence the value of the return from the professional researcher are exactly the same as those that decide your own success.

Information: the more detailed and precise the information you can give, the more likely is it that the searchers will come up with a lot for that £200.

Luck: again our case-histories have underlined the role of luck in these searches – unusual names and, in the earlier records, the quality (or even the existence) of parish records.

Family size: your searchers aim to track down the paternal line and all children of each direct descent marriage. Now if you, sir, in Canada come up with a great-grandfather who had thirteen children, and you, madam, in Australia, with one who had only one child – your grandfather – then there are likely two sequences:

You, sir, will get a large number of relatives on your list, but may feel a little disappointed at the number of generations the searchers have managed to get through.

You, madam, may be very pleased at just how many generation bands the searchers have turned up, but a little disappointed at the lack of 'breadth'.

The tall spindly family tree or the dense squat family bush – you will certainly get a lot of effort from the searchers and they will be trying their hardest to make sure you are pleased with what you get for your money.

Incidentally, if the searchers come up with an 'ancestor' that they cannot fix categorically from documentary evidence, they will end the search and let you know how things stand. You may then accept that while the link cannot be proved it is highly probable – and ask them to continue from the 'ancestor'.

The important point to emphasise is that their work will be ranging not only over the records of New Register House, but also through the legal, land, testamentary material and much else of the neighbouring Scottish Records Office, plus the many directories of apprentices and tradesmen, gravestones and school-rolls, doctors and graduates, churchmen and burgesses.

3. A combination of 1 and 2

It is also worth considering a combination of 1 and 2, where this is possible. You deal directly with the Registrar-General, ordering key documents and building up a partial family tree which you can at some stage hand over to the professionals for their contribution. Similarly – and this is a dimension which has only emerged in recent years – you may get your work from the professional searchers and then do the laborious searching of the OPRs on your own.

All the very best of luck with your attempts to do it from a distance. You will certainly enjoy the experience and it may encourage you, sir, to make that trip from Perth to Scotland, not just to wade through the records, but perhaps to visit those places identified for you in the copies sent to you by the Registrar-General or in the report prepared by your professional searchers. And you, madam, in another Perth, may think it worth coming down to Edinburgh for a couple of days after all!

FOURTEEN

Back Home – Getting it All Down

Now that you have got all that material, what on earth do you do with it?

Over the weeks (months? years?), you will have amassed an enormous hoard of information and at the end of asking a thousand and one questions of who, when and where, you are left with only two: when do I stop, and what do I do then? The first is perhaps the simplest because there is no real answer to it. Genealogy, as I said at the beginning, is a jigsaw puzzle which gets bigger and bigger and which never throws up a piece with an unequivocal straight edge to let you know you've reached the end. And so there is always a temptation to keep searching. At some stage you must resist that temptation and say to yourself: I have reached the stage where I have so much information that I must try and get it down on paper in a manageable form as a record that can clarify my work from my own point of view and that can pass on the fruits of that work to others. Console yourself with the knowledge that this is not an irrevocable decision and any facts which come to light afterwards can be incorporated in all but the most polished finished version. So you've decided to start getting it all down. Pay particular attention to three key aspects:

- putting in order the material you have
- incorporating it into the family tree
- producing a write-up of your findings

Putting in order the material you have collected

The tidy-minded worker will have been keeping a pretty close track of what material he has been accumulating. The owner of a personal computer will have bought very cheaply a suitable genealogy software package and will be able to perform amazing juggling acts at a touch of a key.

Now, however, is the time for everyone to try and shuffle those sheets (or monitor screen pages) into a logical order, file all the census returns together, and mark any cross references on your family or individual sheets. Now is also the time when you should take a careful look at your notepads and information sheets to see if you have missed out any details in transcription or if there are still gaps which can be easily filled.

Building up the family tree

Again, most of you will have been slowly building up a family tree, keeping it simple, using lines and abbreviations as you have seen in the examples in this book. It is now time to try and incorporate all of your material into what is still the most effective way of displaying genealogical information. Each family will pose its own problems as far as layout is concerned, but take a look at history books in your local library and see how other people tackle these challenges.

Get your roughs together and get a clear picture of what your end result should look like. Remember: keep it simple. You are out to produce a device for registering information and passing that information on to others. You are not in the business of producing wallpaper, so cut out the symbolic branches and leafy excesses.

If you intend doing the tree yourself, bear in mind that

the job calls for neatness, patience and dedication as much as artistic inspiration. It also calls for some pretty large sheets of paper. If you have any difficulty in local stationers or artists' materials shops, try any local businesses that you think would be handling such sheets – architects, drawing offices, and, best of all, printers, especially of newspapers who have ideal layout sheets which they may part with in return for courtesy and a smile.

Modern fibre-tip and allied pens provide some ideal writing implements – but check for permanence as you don't want your family tree to dissolve spectacularly when Aunt Mildred weeps over it in memory of her sister Jessie's details. If you are in the slightest doubt, go for the old well-tried Indian ink. You will also find that sticking to black ink will pay dividends when it comes to reproducing copies for distribution within the family

It is always worth remembering that there may be other members of the family who may possess the necessary talents to make an even better job of this part of the exercise and who would be delighted to play a small part in putting your talent for research together with their talents for calligraphy.

The family history takes shape

You have gathered from the bald facts of birth, marriage and death the framework, the skeleton, for your family history. You should also somewhere along the line have been fitting that history into the events of the community and nation in which it took place, with local papers, census returns and such like filling in the details of the grass roots activity and the broader history books telling you something of what was happening in the world around.

You are now ready to build that information into narrative which can be read with interest by other members of the family or (and don't be modest) by people wanting to learn something about a tiny wee segment of Scotland's history as represented by one family.

The easiest and dreariest thing in the world is to rattle off a list of births, marriages and deaths. Take a look at some of those chapters in the New Testament on the lineage of the patriochs and you will be reminded that a chorus of begats is a powerful lullaby indeed.

The following are a few guidelines which might help those of you who are perhaps unused to writing a lengthy continuous report of this type:

1 While it may be that the right way to handle your family history is to start at the earliest date and work through to the present day, take a look at your family tree and see if there is an alternative. You may for example have found far more about one generation than another. If that is Generation Band Six, say, but you had actually traced the family back to Band Ten, don't waste time getting to the interesting bit. Start with your key person and sketch in his background as a sort of flashback.

2 The more you know about Scotland and its history, the better placed you are to slot your forebears into a period, so try some extra background reading now that you know where your forebears lived and what they did. Try and imagine someone in two hundred years' time trying to piece together a history of a family living in Clydeside in the 1940s and not knowing about World War II – and make sure that that is not what you are trying to do when you look back two centuries.

3 Get to know something about the community in which

your family lived. Local newspapers for the nineteenth century and the *Statistical Account* for the eighteenth should get you started. Some of the main locality-based or themed exhibitions and museums should add a bit of style.

4 If you know something of your forebears' occupations, try and find out about what was happening in that trade. Weavers and locomotive-builders, farmers or builders – there are very few people indeed who were working at a job that has been neglected by the academics, writers and publishers of the twentieth century. And as I have already suggested, if you know the name of the company they worked for (and it still exists) try an approach to the company itself.

It may be that you really have difficulty in getting all this together – the amount of information can often deter even the most experienced writer. Again, look at the possibility that someone in the family may have a bent for narrative and a feeling for history. Collaborate with enthusiasm for the sake of the end product.

Finally, just imagine for a moment that you discovered in a dusty chest a bundle of sheets on which your great-great-grandfather had written down a synopsis of his life: his childhood and friends, games and schools, work and courtship, holidays and hobbies, wife and children. Just feel the glee and ponder.

You cannot 'create' that treasure that never was, but you can start laying it down for future generations. Set to it and prepare for the family history the contribution which you can make more fully than anyone in the world – the story of your life, a plain, but not too plain, collection of what you would like your great-great-grandson to know about you. Nothing too grand, not a great autobiographical novel. Although, if you do get hooked . . .

APPENDIX I

General Register Office for Scotland

New Register House, Edinburgh EH1 3YT

Telephone +44 (0)131 314 4433 Fax +44 (0)131 314 4400

www.gro-scotland.gov.uk

at Summer 2005

Copies

A member of staff will search for a specific entry for you – when you have enough information to make identification likely. If the search involves computerised indexes, it will cost you £3 if you go to New Register House or £5 for indexes which are not computerised or if you order by post or fax. If the search is successful, you may then order a copy of the entry (from the post-1855 Births, Marriages and Deaths, from the Old Parochial Records or the census returns) for £8.

Searches

If you want to search the indexes and view records, the charges are as follows:

£10	Part day – unbookable, after 1300 hours
£13	Day – 'off-peak' December to January
£17	Day – 'peak' February to November
£65	One week
£220	Four weeks
£500	One quarter
£1,500	One year

During your search period, you may, at no extra charge, copy details from the entries you identify. If at that time you want 'hard' copy, you can order a certified copy of any entry for £8, ready for collection or posted to you within five days. An uncertified photocopy costs £2.50 and can be ready on the day you order it.

APPENDIX II

Other records in New Register House

A large part of this book has been devoted to the three great treasuries of records kept by the Registrar-General for Scotland. There are, in addition to these and to the excellent array of books on the Library shelves at New Register House, other groups of records of interest to the ancestor-hunter, the first relating to events within Scotland, the others to events outside Scotland.

1. Register of neglected entries
Births, marriages and deaths known to have occurred in Scotland between 1801 and 1854, but not included in the Old Parochial Registers.

2. Marine register of births and deaths after 1855
Births and deaths on British merchant vessels if the child's father or the deceased person was known to be Scottish. (A corresponding register exists for aircraft after 1948.)

3. Service records after 1881
Births, marriages and deaths of Scottish persons at military stations overseas from 1881 to 1959 (army returns), since 1959 (including families and people employed by HM Forces – (service department registers) and certified copies of marriages solemnised by army chaplains outside Britain when at least one party is described as Scottish and at least one serving in HM Forces.

4. War registers from 1899
Deaths of serving men recorded in the registers for the South African (1899-1902), 1914-18 and 1939-45 wars.

5. Consular returns
Births (from 1914), marriages (from 1917) and deaths (from 1914) registered by British consuls.

6. Foreign countries
Births of children of Scottish parents, marriages and deaths of Scottish subjects, from information supplied by the parties concerned.

APPENDIX III

Names and the ancestor-hunter

Surnames or family names have in their derivations little to offer to the ancestor-hunter. They were formed perhaps five centuries before the period that most of you will be studying. In most cases, of course, surnames sprang up all over Britain independently of one another, and while it is of interest to, say, the bearers of the most common surname in England and Scotland to know that the first 'Smith' was recorded in Durham, that fact has no genealogical significance whatsoever

Even when a name is extremely localised – as in the case of one derived from an estate – this location will have little or no significance as a link in your own searches. My wife's family, for example, took their name from the small estate of Balbirnie in Fife. The last member of the family to own the estate had moved out before 1500, while the earliest one bearing the name which we have managed to link as a direct ancestor was flourishing in Edinburgh around 1750. Clearly it is fanciful to draw in a long line connecting the two.

Even where the great clan names have strong territorial links, the nineteenth century knew no such limits, for by then Highlanders had spread throughout Scotland and indeed the world. Certainly one would find very many Macdonalds in the Hebrides, but equally certainly your unidentified great-grandfather Donald Macdonald could have been living anywhere in Scotland from John o' Groats to Gretna Green before he left for Canada in 1860.

And as we have seen in the book, spelling conventions have nothing like the significance we attribute to them today, so the fact that you spell your name 'Miller' and not 'Millar' may have no bearing whatsoever on a grandfather who may have used either spelling – or never found any need to spell it at all.

Christian names, or more correctly given names, can, on the other hand, prove extremely useful to the ancestor-hunter. The Scots adopted a traditional, almost ritual, attitude to the naming of children. Not for them the scanning of books on boys' names and girls' names when the newcomer appeared, no Brad or Poppy, Clint or Kylie for them. Babies were named after relatives and the happy couple who departed from a rigid set of priorities did so at their peril and with a great risk of family friction at the least and disinheritance at the most extreme. The list went something like this:

Sons: 1 – father's father; 2 – mother's father; 3 – father

Daughters: 1 – mother's mother; 2 – father's mother; 3 – mother

This 'pecking order' as far as the naming of the new baby is concerned cannot be presented as a fixed, no-exception formula. There were occasional regional variations, where sometimes two or even three of the people in the list bore the same name, and, sometimes, a recent death might push someone to the front of the naming queue.

Study your family's name patterns carefully, especially in the earlier years, and you will often find them giving you valuable pointers. When you come across a new name, look very hard indeed at the circumstances; it will almost certainly mean something, perhaps only the fact that a long run of boys or girls has used up the stock of traditional family Christian names.

While spelling of given names is usually more consistent than that of surnames, bear in mind that there can be variations not only in form (Ian/John, Hamish/James) but also in contractions. A Marion or an Alison may be called Mary or Ann and pass on the name to the next generation in this new form.

The downside of the rigid naming structure is obvious and very few of you will avoid it completely. Let's imagine that Alexander Peattie had four sons, all of whom in turn have a son. Then there would be four boys, all cousins, bearing the same name of Alexander Peattie. Once you're into state records there should be no problem distinguishing one from the other, but in earlier times can you really be sure you have the right man?

Today, this pattern is changing and it is not so necessary to identify the many Alexanders in the family by a host of additives, from Big Sandy to Davy's Sandy, from Alex to Alick. In its place, alas, we have a range of strange rootless names providing variety but dissolving links.

APPENDIX IV

The regularity of irregular marriages

Up until 1940, Scotland had a distinctive form of marriage, known rather imprecisely as an irregular marriage. This, the so-called Gretna Green marriage which lured panting English lovers north of the Border pursued by grey-beard kinsmen brandishing swords, was a perfectly acceptable alternative to the conventional church wedding, involving instead a declaration in front of witnesses or before a sheriff. The epithet 'irregular' should not lead you to believe that it was illegal or second rate (it wasn't), or that it was indulged in by a small minority. One senior member of staff in the Registrar General's office pointed out to me that in checking through the first 200 marriages in Glasgow Blythswood for 1904, he counted 81, more than 40 per cent, which were marriages by declaration.

By the Marriage (Scotland) Act 1939, the alternative to a church wedding became a new form of civil marriage contracted in the office and presence of certain specially authorised Registrars after publication of notice.

APPENDIX V

Illegitimacy – a hurdle for the ancestor-hunter

A friend of mine started to tell me of a family tradition, but before mentioning any details he stopped and asked me to look into his forebears and see if I came up with anything unusual. Intrigued, I did as he asked and went speedily back three or four generations without a hiccup. Then I came across an ancestor who posed some problems which eventually boiled down to three different pairs of parents given on his marriage certificate, his death certificate and, after a long search, his birth certificate. And no one name appeared twice! No man has six parents, so I had to dream up some tale of passion, unrequited love and illegitimacy which coincided quite closely with the family tradition. My friend went one better by revealing that his family tradition held that none of the three fathers was correct!

That was perhaps an extreme case of what illegitimacy can do to the ancestor-hunter. At the worst, it can bring an abrupt end to the male or even in the case of a foundling to both lines, with little or no chance of further progress. At the mildest, it can introduce new elements into the search. It is quite common for ancestor-hunters to come across illegitimacy at some time. Just consider the following two instances as a sample of what you should bear in mind if your searches seem to be coming up against a brick wall:

1. A child might be born illegitimate and the mother might persuade the father to acknowledge paternity and give the child his name. A later separation or failure to reach the altar might mean the child reverting to the mother's name or indeed acquiring the name of her future husband.

Symptom: one name on the birth certificate, a second on marriage and death certificates.

2. The mother might not be able to get the father to give his name to the child and the baptismal/birth entry would be made in the mother's name. The couple might subsequently marry and legitimise the child.

Symptom: the same as previously but with the names reversed.

If you come across an illegitimate birth where no father's name is given, you may be able to make progress by a paternity suit (the Corrected Entry shown on the birth certificate) or a mention in the session records. If the village grapevine knew who the father was, it would soon have got through to the kirk elders.

APPENDIX VI

Six of the best – great websites you cannot miss

www.familysearch.org
The great site from the Church of Jesus Christ of Latter Day Saints. Unchallenged for adding to your own tree, making contact with other searchers, ordering LDS products and getting a real feel for genealogy.

www.origins.net
Straight into the great indexes of the GRO. A charge is levied but enormous value for money, and you can order copies from GRO.

www.genuki.org
The best and easiest way into the riches of the world wide web.

www.scottishmuseums.org
Because I believe that getting along to, say, the canal museum in West Lothian and then popping over for lunch and a beer at the Bridge Inn and a canal trip is just as relevant to family research as reading a monograph on canal developments in Central Scotland. And much more fun.

www.nas.gov.uk
The easiest way to get to know just what riches are on offer at the National Archives of Scotland. Plenty of useful factsheets to download.

www.scotsgenealogy.com
To let you see what a contribution the Scottish Genealogy Society has made to this greatest of hobbies – and to make sure you see the amazing array of publications they have created and don't miss the one that's targeted at you.

You will find more – existing websites are continually changing, and new ones are being created. A major new genealogy and tourism site has recently been launched at www.ancestralscotland.com by VisitScotland (formerly Scottish Tourist Board).

Some other books published by **LUATH** PRESS

A Passion for Scotland

David R. Ross

ISBN 1 84282 019 2 PBK £5.99

David R. Ross is passionate about Scotland's past. And its future. In this heartfelt journey through Scotland's story, he shares his passion for what it means to be a Scot.

Eschewing xenophobia, his deep understanding of how Scotland's history touches her people shines through. All over Scotland, into England and Europe, over to Canada, Chicago and Washington – the people and the places that bring Scotland's story to life, and death – including

The Early Scots
Wallace and Bruce
The Union
Montrose
The Jacobites
John MacLean
Tartan Day USA

and, revealed for the first time, the burial places of all Scotland's monarchs.

This is not a history book. But it covers history.

This is not a travel guide. But some places mentioned might be worth a visit.

This is not a political manifesto. But a personal one.

Read this book. It might make you angry. It might give you hope. You might shed a tear. You might not agree with David R. Ross.

But read this book. You might rediscover your roots, your passion for Scotland.

'The biker-historian's unique combination of unabashed romanticism and easy irreverence make him the ideal guide to historical subjects all too easily swallowed up in maudlin sentiment or 'demythologized' by the academic studies.'
THE SCOTSMAN

'Ross writes with an immediacy, a dynamism, that makes his subjects come alive on the page.'
DUNDEE COURIER

'A fresh, honest approach... Ross is unashamedly proud to be Scottish.' DUMFRIES AND GALLOWAY STANDARD

Desire Lines: A Scottish Odyssey

David R. Ross

ISBN 1 84282 033 8 PBK £9.99

A must read for every Scot, everyone living in Scotland and everyone visiting Scotland!

David R Ross not only shows us his Scotland but he teaches us it too. You feel as though you are on the back of his motorcycle listening to the stories of his land as you fly with him up and down the smaller roads, the 'desire lines', of Scotland. Ross takes us off the beaten track and away from the main routes chosen for us by modern road builders.

He starts our journey in England and criss-crosses the border telling the bloody tales of the towns and villages. His recounting of Scottish history, its myths and its legends is unapologetically and unashamedly pro-Scots.

His tour takes us northwards towards Edinburgh through Athelstaneford, the place where the Saltire was born. From there we head to the Forth valley and on into the Highlands and beyond, taking in the stories of the villains and heroes through Scottish history.

Pride and passion for his country, the people, the future of Scotland; and his uncompromising patriotism shines through *Desire Lines*, David R Ross's homage to his beloved country.

Scotlands of the Mind

Angus Calder

ISBN 1 84282 008 7 PBK £9.99

Does Scotland as a 'nation' have any real existence? In Britain, in Europe, in the World? Or are there a multitude of multiform 'Scotlands of the Mind'?

These soul-searching questions are probed in this timely book by prize-winning author and journalist, Angus Calder. Informed and intelligent, this new volume presents the author at his thought-provoking best. The absorbing journey through many possible Scotlands – fictionalised, idealised, and politicised – is sure to fascinate.

This perceptive and often highly personal writing shows the breathtaking scope of Calder's analytical power. Fact or fiction, individual or international, politics or poetry, statistics or statehood, no subject is taboo in a volume that offers an overview of the vicissitudes and changing nature of Scottishness.

Through mythical times to manufactured histories, from Empire and Diaspora, from John Knox to Home Rule and beyond, Calder shatters literary, historical and cultural misconceptions and provides invaluable insights into the Scottish psyche. Offering a fresh understanding of an ever-evolving Scotland, *Scotlands of the Mind* contributes to what Calder himself has called 'the needful getting of a new act together'.

Notes from the North incorporating a Brief History of the Scots and the English

Emma Wood

ISBN 1 84282 048 6 PBK £7.99

Notes on being English
Notes on being in Scotland
Learning from a shared past

Sickened by the English jingoism that surfaced in rampant form during the 1982 Falklands War, Emma Wood started to dream of moving from her home in East Anglia to the Highlands of Scotland. She felt increasingly frustrated and marginalised as Thatcherism got a grip on the southern English psyche. The Scots she met on frequent holidays in the Highlands had no truck with Thatcherism, and she felt at home with grass-roots Scottish anti-authoritarianism. The decision was made. She uprooted and headed for a new life in the north of Scotland.

'An intelligent and perceptive book... calm, reflective, witty and sensitive. It should certainly be read by all English visitors to Scotland, be they tourists or incomers. And it should certainly be read by all Scots concerned about what kind of nation we live in. They might learn something about themselves.'

THE HERALD

'... her enlightenment is evident on every page of this perceptive, provocative book.'

MAIL ON SUNDAY

Luath Scots Language Learner

An introduction to contemporary spoken Scots

L Colin Wilson

ISBN 0 946487 91 X pbk £9.99
ISBN 1 84282 026 5 double CD £16.99

25 graded lessons; English-to-Scots vocabulary list; verb tables; dialogues; grammatical explanations; exercises; background information about life in Scotland; cultural context

The first-ever Scots language course, suitable as an introductory course or for those interested in re-acquainting themselves with the language of childhood and grandparents.

'This gies us whit dictionars niver will gie, a taste o the richt idiom o the thing.'

JOHN LAW, SCOTS LANGUAGE RESOURCE CENTRE

The Luath Burns Companion

John Cairney

ISBN 1 84282 000 1 PBK £10.00

'Robert Burns was born in a thunderstorm and lived his brief life by flashes of lightning.'

So says John Cairney in his introduction. In those flashes his genius revealed itself.

This collection is not another 'complete works' but a personal selection from 'The Man Who Played Robert Burns'. This is very much John's book. His favourites are reproduced here and he talks about them with an obvious love of the man and his work. His depth of knowledge and understanding has been garnered over forty years of study, writing and performance.

The collection includes sixty poems, songs and other works; and an essay that explores Burns's life and influences, his triumphs and tragedies. This informed introduction provides the reader with an insight into Burns's world.

Burns's work has drama, passion, pathos and humour. His careful workmanship is concealed by the spontaneity of his verse. He was always a forward thinking man and remains a writer for the future.

FICTION

Lord of Illusions
Dilys Rose
ISBN 1 84282 076 1 PBK £7.99

Torch
Lin Anderson
ISBN 1 84282 042 7 PBK £9.99

Heartland
John MacKay
ISBN 1 84282 059 1 PBK £9.99

The Blue Moon Book
Anne MacLeod
ISBN 1 84282 061 3 PBK £9.99

The Glasgow Dragon
Des Dillon
ISBN 1 84282 056 7 PBK £9.99

But n Ben A-Go-Go
Matthew Fitt
ISBN 0 946487 82 0 HB £10.99
ISBN 1 84282 014 1 PB £6.99

CURRENT ISSUES

Notes from the North incorporating a Brief History of the Scots and the English
Emma Wood
ISBN 1 84282 048 6 PBK £7.99

Trident on Trial the case for people's disarmament
Angie Zelter
ISBN 1 84282 004 4 PBK £9.99

Broomie Law
Cinders McLeod
ISBN 0 946487 99 5 PBK £4.00

TRAVEL & LEISURE

Pilgrims in the Rough: St Andrews beyond the 19th Hole
Michael Tobert
ISBN 0 946487 74 X PBK £7.99

Let's Explore Edinburgh Old Town
Anne Bruce English
ISBN 0 946487 98 7 PBK £4.99

LUATH GUIDES TO SCOTLAND

Mull and Iona: Highways and Byways
Peter Macnab
ISBN 0 946487 58 8 PBK £4.95

The West Highlands: The Lonely Lands
Tom Atkinson
ISBN 0 946487 56 1 PBK £4.95

The Northern Highlands: The Empty Lands
Tom Atkinson
ISBN 0 946487 55 3 PBK £4.95

The North West Highlands: Roads to the Isles
Tom Atkinson
ISBN 0 946487 54 5 PBK £4.95

WALK WITH LUATH

Mountain Days & Bothy Nights
Dave Brown and Ian Mitchell
ISBN 0 946487 15 4 PBK £7.50

The Joy of Hillwalking
Ralph Storer
ISBN 1 84282 069 9 PBK £7.50

Scotland's Mountains before the Mountaineers
Ian Mitchell
ISBN 0 946487 39 1 PBK £9.99

LUATH WALKING GUIDES

Walks in the Cairngorms
Ernest Cross
ISBN 0 946487 09 X PBK £4.95

Short Walks in the Cairngorms
Ernest Cross
ISBN 0 946487 23 5 PBK £4.95

ON THE TRAIL OF

On the Trail of William Wallace
David R. Ross
ISBN 0 946487 47 2 PBK £7.99

On the Trail of Scotland's Myths and Legends
Stuart McHardy
ISBN 1 84282 049 4 PBK £7.99

On the Trail of Robert the Bruce
David R. Ross
ISBN 0 946487 52 9 PBK £7.99

On the Trail of Mary Queen of Scots
J. Keith Cheetham
ISBN 0 946487 50 2 PBK £7.99

On the Trail of Bonnie Prince Charlie
David R. Ross
ISBN 0 946487 68 5 PBK £7.99

On the Trail of John Muir
Cherry Good
ISBN 0 946487 62 6 PBK £7.99

On the Trail of The Pilgrim Fathers
J. Keith Cheetham
ISBN 0 946487 83 9 PBK £7.99

On the Trail of Queen Victoria in the Highlands
Ian R. Mitchell
ISBN 0 946487 79 0 PBK £7.99

HISTORY

Reportage Scotland: Scotland's history in the voices of those who were there
Louise Yeoman
ISBN 1 84282 051 6 PBK £6.99

The Quest for Arthur
Stuart McHardy
ISBN 1 84282 012 5 HBK £16.99

The Quest for the Celtic Key
Karen Ralls-Macleod
Ian Robertson
ISBN 0 946487 73 1 HBK £18.99

SOCIAL HISTORY

Pumpherston: the story of a shale oil village
Sybil Cavanagh
ISBN 1 84282 011 7 HB £17.99
ISBN 1 84282 015 X PB £10.99

Hail Philpstoun's Queen
Barbara and Marie Pattullo
ISBN 1 84282 095 8 PB £6.99

Shale Voices
Alistair Findlay
foreword by Tam Dalyell MP
ISBN 0 946487 63 4 PBK £10.99
ISBN 0 946487 78 2 HBK £17.99

Crofting Years
Francis Thompson
ISBN 0 946487 06 5 PBK £6.95

A Word for Scotland
Jack Campbell
foreword by Magnus Magnusson
ISBN 0 946487 48 0 PBK £12.99

FOLKLORE

The Supernatural Highlands
Francis Thompson
ISBN 0 946487 31 6 PBK £8.99

Tall Tales from an Island
Peter Macnab
ISBN 0 946487 07 3 PBK £8.99

Tales from the North Coast
Alan Temperley
ISBN 0 946487 18 9 PBK £8.99

Highland Myths & Legends
George W Macpherson
ISBN 1 84282 003 6 PBK £5.00

SPORT

Over the Top with the Tartan Army (Active Service 1992-97)
Andrew McArthur
ISBN 0 946487 45 6 PBK £7.99

FOOD AND DRINK

The Whisky Muse
Scotch Whisky in Poem and Song
Collected and introduced by Robin Laing
Illustrated by Bob Dewar
ISBN 0 946487 95 2 PBK £12.99

Edinburgh and Leith Pub Guide
Stuart McHardy
ISBN 0 946487 80 4 PBK £4.95

NATURAL SCOTLAND

Wild Scotland: The essential guide to finding the best of natural Scotland
James McCarthy
Photography by Laurie Campbell
ISBN 0 946487 37 5 PBK £8.99

Scotland Land and People
An Inhabited Solitude
James McCarthy
ISBN 0 946487 57 X PBK £7.99

The Highland Geology Trail
John L Roberts
ISBN 0 946487 36 7 PBK £4.99

Rum: Nature's Island
Magnus Magnusson
ISBN 0 946487 32 4 PBK £7.95

Red Sky at Night
John Barrington
ISBN 0 946487 60 X PBK £8.99

Listen to the Trees
Don MacCaskill
ISBN 0 946487 65 0 PBK £9.99

Wildlife: Otters – On the Swirl of the Tide
Bridget MacCaskill
ISBN 0 946487 67 7 PBK £9.99

Wildlife: Foxes – The Blood is Wild
Bridget MacCaskill
ISBN 0 946487 71 5 PBK £9.99

BIOGRAPHY

Tobermory Teuchter: A first-hand account of life on Mull in the early years of the 20th century
Peter Macnab
ISBN 0 946487 41 3 PBK £7.99

Bare Feet and Tackety Boots
Archie Cameron
ISBN 0 946487 17 0 PBK £7.95

The Last Lighthouse
Sharma Kraustopf
ISBN 0 946487 96 0 PBK £7.99

POETRY

Burning Whins
Liz Niven
ISBN 1 84282 074 5 PB £8.99

Drink the Green Fairy
Brian Whittingham
ISBN 1 84282 020 6 PB £8.99

Tartan & Turban
Bashabi Fraser
ISBN 1 84282 044 3 PB £8.99

The Ruba'iyat of Omar Khayyam, in Scots
Rab Wilson
ISBN 1 84282 046 X PB £8.99

Talking with Tongues
Brian D. Finch
ISBN 1 84282 006 0 PB £8.99

Picking Brambles
Des Dillon
ISBN 1 84282 021 4 PB £6.99

Sex, Death & Football
Alistair Findlay
ISBN 1 84282 022 2 PB £6.99

Luath Press Limited

committed to publishing well written books worth reading

LUATH PRESS takes its name from Robert Burns, whose little collie Luath (*Gael.*, swift or nimble) tripped up Jean Armour at a wedding and gave him the chance to speak to the woman who was to be his wife and the abiding love of his life. Burns called one of *The Twa Dogs* Luath after Cuchullin's hunting dog in *Ossian's Fingal*. Luath Press was established in 1981 in the heart of Burns country, and is now based a few steps up the road from Burns' first lodgings on Edinburgh's Royal Mile.
Luath offers you distinctive writing with a hint of unexpected pleasures.

Most bookshops in the UK, the US, Canada, Australia, New Zealand and parts of Europe either carry our books in stock or can order them for you. To order direct from us, please send a £sterling cheque, postal order, international money order or your credit card details (number, address of cardholder and expiry date) to us at the address below. Please add post and packing as follows: UK – £1.00 per delivery address; overseas surface mail – £2.50 per delivery address; overseas airmail – £3.50 for the first book to each delivery address, plus £1.00 for each additional book by airmail to the same address. If your order is a gift, we will happily enclose your card or message at no extra charge.

ILLUSTRATION: IAN KELLAS

Luath Press Limited
543/2 Castlehill
The Royal Mile
Edinburgh EH1 2ND
Scotland
Telephone: 0131 225 4326 (24 hours)
Fax: 0131 225 4324
email: gavin.macdougall@luath.co.uk
Website: www.luath.co.uk